# Get the most from this book

Everyone has to decide his or her own revision strategy, but it is essential to review your work, learn it and test your understanding. These Revision Notes will help you to do that in a planned way, topic by topic. Use this book as the cornerstone of your revision and don't hesitate to write in it — personalise your notes and check your progress by ticking off each section as you revise.

### ✓ Tick to track your progress

Use the revision planner on pages 4 and 5 to plan your revision, topic by topic. Tick each box when you have:

- revised and understood a topic
- tested yourself
- practised the exam questions and gone online to check your answers and complete the quick quizzes

You can also keep track of you. each topic heading in the book. You may find it helpful to add your own notes as you work through each topic.

## My revision planner

**Unit 1 Introduction to critical thinking**

| | | Revised | Tested | Gone online |
|---|---|---|---|---|
| 1 | The language of reasoning | | | |
| 7 | Analysis | ☐ | ☐ | ☐ |
| 11 | Evaluation | ☐ | ☐ | ☐ |
| 2 | Credibility | | | |

## Analysis

**Identifying an argument** ———————————— Revised ☐

The first few questions of the Unit 1 examination ask you to analyse the structure of an **argument** by identifying various **components** or **elements**. This means that you need to understand and memorise vocabulary, and use it precisely.

**Arguments** are attempts to persuade, containing reasons and a conclusion. Indicator words often help to distinguish these two components or elements. If in

# Features to help you succeed

### Exam tips and summaries

Throughout the book there are tips from the examiner to help you boost your final grade.

Summaries provide advice on how to approach each topic in the exams, and suggest other things you might want to mention to gain those valuable extra marks.

### Definitions and key words

Clear, concise definitions of essential key terms are provided on the page where they appear.

Key words from the specification are highlighted in bold for you throughout the book.

### Now test yourself

These short, knowledge-based questions provide the first step in testing your learning. Answers are at the end of the book.

### Typical mistakes

The author identifies the typical mistakes candidates make and explains how you can avoid them.

### Check your understanding

Use these questions at the end of each section to make sure that you have understood every topic. Answers are at the end of the book.

### Exam practice

Practice exam questions are provided for each topic. Use them to consolidate your revision and practise your exam skills.

### Online

Go online to check and print your answers to the exam questions and try out the extra quick quizzes at **www.therevisionbutton.co.uk/myrevisionnotes**

# My revision planner

Exam practice answers and quick quizzes at **www.therevisionbutton.co.uk/myrevisionnotes**

Exam practice answers and quick quizzes at **www.therevisionbutton.co.uk/myrevisionnotes**

# Countdown to my exams

## 6–8 weeks to go

- Start by looking at the specification — make sure you know exactly what material you need to revise and the style of the examination. Use the revision planner on pages 4 and 5 to familiarise yourself with the topics.
- Organise your notes, making sure you have covered everything on the specification. The revision planner will help you to group your notes into topics.
- Work out a realistic revision plan that will allow you time for relaxation. Set aside days and times for all the subjects that you need to study, and stick to your timetable.
- Set yourself sensible targets. Break your revision down into focused sessions of around 40 minutes, divided by breaks. These Revision Notes organise the basic facts into short, memorable sections to make revising easier.

Revised ☐

## 4–6 weeks to go

- Read through the relevant sections of this book and refer to the exam tips, exam summaries, typical mistakes and key terms. Tick off the topics as you feel confident about them. Highlight those topics you find difficult and look at them again in detail.
- Test your understanding of each topic by working through the 'Now test yourself' and 'Check your understanding' questions in the book. Look up the answers at the back of the book.
- Make a note of any problem areas as you revise, and ask your teacher to go over these in class.
- Look at past papers. They are one of the best ways to revise and practise your exam skills. Write or prepare planned answers to the exam practice questions provided in this book. Check your answers online and try out the extra quick quizzes at **www.therevisionbutton.co.uk/ myrevisionnotes**
- Try different revision methods. For example, you can make notes using mind maps, spider diagrams or flash cards.
- Track your progress using the revision planner and give yourself a reward when you have achieved your target.

Revised ☐

## One week to go

- Try to fit in at least one more timed practice of an entire past paper and seek feedback from your teacher, comparing your work closely with the mark scheme.
- Check the revision planner to make sure you haven't missed out any topics. Brush up on any areas of difficulty by talking them over with a friend or getting help from your teacher.
- Attend any revision classes put on by your teacher. Remember, he or she is an expert at preparing people for examinations.

Revised ☐

## The day before the examination

- Flick through these Revision Notes for useful reminders, for example the exam tips, exam summaries, typical mistakes and key terms.
- Check the time and place of your examination.
- Make sure you have everything you need — extra pens and pencils, tissues, a watch, bottled water, sweets.
- Allow some time to relax and have an early night to ensure you are fresh and alert for the examinations.

Revised ☐

## My exams

**AS Critical Thinking Unit 1**

Date: .................................................................................

Time: .................................................................................

Location: ...........................................................................

**AS Critical Thinking Unit 2**

Date: .................................................................................

Time: .................................................................................

Location: ...........................................................................

**A2 Critical Thinking Unit 3**

Date: .................................................................................

Time: .................................................................................

Location: ...........................................................................

**A2 Critical Thinking Unit 4**

Date: .................................................................................

Time: .................................................................................

Location: ...........................................................................

# 1 The language of reasoning

## Analysis

### Identifying an argument

Revised

The first few questions of the Unit 1 examination ask you to analyse the structure of an **argument** by identifying various **components** or **elements**. This means that you need to understand and memorise vocabulary, and use it precisely.

An argument is a written or spoken attempt to convince or persuade, using reasons to support the conclusion. In critical thinking, expressions of opinion not backed up by reasons are not called arguments. For example:

> As rail travel is less damaging to the environment than air travel (R), tourists should be encouraged to take trains instead of planes (C).

The first part is the reason (R) and the last part is the conclusion (C). The word 'should' indicates an attempt at persuasion.

A conclusion does not necessarily come at the end of an argument. Consider this example:

> Tourists should be encouraged to take trains instead of planes (C) because rail travel is less damaging to the environment than air travel (R).

Verbal clues, known as **argument indicators**, can sometimes help to distinguish conclusions from reasons.

Conclusions are often preceded by the **conclusion indicators** *therefore, so, consequently, hence* or *thus*. They may include words such as *must, should, need* or *ought to* if they are recommending some course of action.

Reasons are often preceded by **reason indicators** such as *because, for, as* and *since*.

Where there is no indicator word, you have to work out from the context which parts of the argument consist of reasons and which part is the conclusion that can be drawn from the reasons. For example:

> Rats make good pets. They can quickly be taught to perform tricks.

If unsure, apply the *therefore* test. Try the conclusion indicator word *therefore* or *so* and then the reason indicator word *because* between the two sentences above, to see which fits the context. *Because* fits best, so the first sentence is the conclusion.

Arguments can be supported by one or more reasons, as in this example:

> Universities prefer students to study more than three AS subjects (R1), so you should add critical thinking to your other choices (C). The skills will be particularly helpful if you intend to do LNAT, UKCAT or BMAT tests (R2).

**Arguments** are attempts to persuade, containing reasons and a conclusion. Indicator words often help to distinguish these two components or elements. If in doubt, apply the *therefore* test.

**Now test yourself**

1  Which is the conclusion here? Critical thinking must be a good test of intelligence. Our students' grades relate closely to their IQ scores.

Tested

Notice the use of the **notations** (abbreviations) for the **components** of the argument, R1, R2 and C, which the examination board encourages you to use.

A statement made without giving a reason is called an **assertion** or a **claim**. It may be an attempt to persuade or an expression of opinion such as:

> Gordon Brown was a good prime minister.

This conclusion is weakened by the lack of supporting reasons.

The word **claim** is also used when witnesses make statements about what they have seen or done or about their innocence or someone else's guilt. They make **claims** in court or when interviewed by the media. For example:

> I saw the soldiers shoot indiscriminately into the crowd.

**Explanations** also differ from arguments. Although they often have reasons and conclusions, they do not attempt to persuade. They may provide evidence to support statements already accepted as facts by public consensus. For example:

> You will need to alter your watch when you go to France because of the time difference of 1 hour.

In the passages in critical thinking examinations, explanations sometimes set the scene, or clarify a situation, and may then be followed by an argument. For example:

> Education Maintenance Allowances were originally introduced because students from poorer families found it difficult to manage without paid work. It is wrong that the current government...

> Unlike arguments, **claims** or **assertions** are not supported by reasons. **Explanations** differ from arguments in not attempting to persuade.

## Counter-claims and counter-arguments

Revised

Most of the material in an argument comprises reasons, evidence and examples supporting the main conclusion.

A brief contrary statement that is introduced without its backing reasons is called a **counter-assertion** or **counter-claim**. An argument against biofuels might begin as follows:

> Many people think biofuels are the answer to the environmental crisis, but they are sadly mistaken.

The words before the comma state the counter-claim, which is immediately challenged. This response to the counter-claim can be viewed as a reason supporting the main argument and is likely to be followed by further reasons why relying on biofuels is a mistake.

A **counter-argument** is usually longer than a counter-claim, because it provides supporting reasons. Each reason might then be dismissed in turn to support the main conclusion of the argument. You may be asked to identify the counter-conclusion and the counter-reasons that make up the counter-argument.

> **Exam tip**
>
> The indicator word 'although' often flags up a counter-claim or counter-argument.

> A **counter-argument** opposes the main argument and states why, so it consists of a counter-conclusion and one or more counter-reasons, whereas **counter-claims** and **counter-assertions** provide no reasons.

## Now test yourself

2 Identify the counter-argument (CA) in the passage that follows.

The government should think twice about attempting to increase the time devoted to sports at school. Forcing reluctant teenagers to participate in outdoor team games in freezing weather can put them off sport for life. Some defend school sports because exercise counteracts obesity and strengthens the bones of the young. However, encouraging youngsters to walk briskly to school every day would be more beneficial on both these counts than the physical activity a reluctant student is likely to participate in on the sports field. Improved education about diet could also do more to build healthy bodies than compulsory sport.

## Distinguishing reasons from evidence and examples — Revised ☐

The conclusions of longer arguments are usually drawn from a number of reasons, which may be supported by **evidence** (Ev) and **examples** (Ex).

Students often confuse evidence, examples and reasons.

- Reasons are the general points supporting the conclusion.
- Evidence often consists of research findings, statistics and experts' opinions that substantiate a reason.
- Examples are specific instances supporting a reason.

**Exam tip**

To help you distinguish evidence from reasons, think about how you would create a brief summary of the argument, excluding evidence but not reasons or conclusion.

## Now test yourself

3 Analyse the passage below to identify the conclusion, reasons and evidence.

Fathers should be permitted to stay overnight in post-natal wards and medical staff should involve them more in the care of their newborn babies. A man's sense of responsibility for his child tends to be weakened if he feels excluded straight after the birth. According to the Fatherhood Institute, maternity hospitals frequently emphasise the mother's responsibility for the newborn baby but give the father the impression that he is not needed in the hospital. Fathers often lack information about caring for babies, which they could easily learn from the hospital staff. In a MORI survey for Mothercare, only 3% of males correctly answered four basic questions about looking after newborn babies.

## Hypothetical reasoning — Revised ☐

Reasons are always put forward as being true, but may prove to be unconvincing. Arguments can be supported by reasons based on observations, accepted facts, opinions, research data, eyewitness testimonies or hypothetical reasoning.

**Hypothetical reasoning** is often based on what may result from possible future conditions. This type of reasoning, often signalled by the indicators *if* and *then*, can be challenged as there is no certainty about future events.

**Hypothetical reasoning** may predict a particular outcome if a condition is achieved. Alternatively it speculates what the outcome would have been if an event in the past had been different. Both may be examples of poor reasoning.

## Now test yourself

4 Evaluate the hypothetical reasoning below:

If new fathers are allowed to stay with the mothers and babies in maternity hospitals, then they will take more responsibility for their children in the long term.

Look out for speculations about the future, even if the actual words 'if' and 'then' are absent. For example:

> The government is intending to prolong compulsory education and training to the age of 18. Should this happen, British workers will be better qualified to compete with foreigners seeking work here.

An even weaker type of hypothetical reasoning is about the past, supposing what would have happened if events had been different. For example:

> If the atomic bomb had not been invented, fewer people would have died in the Second World War.

This argument is flawed because if one past event had been different, then so might many others. Past events are already established facts so speculating about how they could have turned out differently cannot be based on evidence and is poor reasoning, however interesting it may be.

## Assumptions

Revised ☐

An **assumption**, sometimes known as a **supposition**, is an unstated part of the argument — something that is taken for granted and not mentioned directly, often because it seems obvious to the arguer. There are no indicator words preceding assumptions because they are not explicit, so they require some thought to identify. For example:

> Boys may often be less successful at school than girls because, as research shows, their concentration span is shorter.

Here an assumption is made that the research mentioned compared the concentration of girls and boys of the same age and in identical conditions.

> **Assumptions** are hidden suppositions acting as reasons to support a conclusion.

## Exam tip

To test that you have correctly identified an assumption, apply the reverse or negative test. By changing the assumption to its opposite (e.g. 'Girls' and boys' concentration was tested in different conditions') you should find that the conclusion can no longer be reached.

Remember that nothing that is written in the document can possibly be an assumption.

In everyday language people sometimes use the word 'assumption' for a statement that the speaker thinks is true but others disagree about. For example:

> Men are better at map-reading than women.

However, in critical thinking such a broad and unsubstantiated claim would be called a sweeping generalisation (see Unit 2). It cannot be an assumption because it is written down.

### Now test yourself

5  Identify several assumptions in the following:

My student son is coming home for the Easter holidays. He will be disappointed unless I make time to go out and buy him a big Easter egg.

Tested ☐

## Tips for analysing arguments

Revised ☐

● When asked to identify components or elements of arguments, quote the author's exact words: 2 or 3 marks are awarded for accurate quotation and fewer marks if you write it in your own words to demonstrate understanding or save time. Remember that critical thinking requires great precision of expression.

- An exception to exact copying is if the quoted phrase has a pronoun in it. Replace words such as 'it' or 'they' with the appropriate noun to make complete sense of the statement. Words that indicate the direction of the argument, such as 'however' and 'moreover', may also be omitted if quoting components such as counter-arguments or reasons.

- Ensure that you do not quote more than the component required. If asked to identify a reason in a passage, exclude any examples and evidence embedded within it. A reason for banning drugs might be presented in the text as follows:

> Many illegal drugs, such as cannabis, are believed to affect the memory.

You would need to write out:

> Many illegal drugs are believed to affect the memory.

as the rest of the sentence is an example.

- Do not confuse evidence with reasons. Generally speaking, each paragraph is likely to contain a reason supported by some evidence or examples. The reason is an essential broad point and the evidence and examples more illustrative, mentioning specific people, places or data.

- Use highlighters or pencil underlining to identify main components of arguments and to underline flaws in reasoning you notice as you first read the passage.

- As well as identifying components, be prepared to explain how you have recognised them from their role in the argument. Learning definitions carefully will help with this.

If the conclusion stated in the passage was:

'Smoking should be strongly discouraged.'

you would lose marks if you wrote:

'Smoking should be discouraged.'

You will not gain marks for answers where you try to save time by using an ellipsis to indicate words missing in the middle of a quotation, for example 'Smoking...discouraged.'

# Evaluation

Part of Unit 1 requires you to judge how strongly the reasoning in a passage supports the conclusion, expressing your assessment using technical terms. This includes identifying assumptions that may be unjustified or evidence that is unrepresentative or inadequate. (Detailed knowledge of more flaws in reasoning is required for Unit 2.)

## Assessing assumptions

**Revised**

To assess the reasonableness of an assumption, decide whether it assumes some factual point that could be established.

> Girls are doing so much better than boys in school subjects that soon all the best jobs will be taken by females.

Here the assumption being made is:

> There is a high correlation between school qualifications and level of employment subsequently obtained.

You could write that the soundness of this assumption could be checked but that the information was not presented in the passage.

Alternatively the assumption might be based on an opinion, e.g.

> Girls are doing so much better than boys in school subjects that soon employers will have to positively discriminate in favour of male employees.

An assumption here, in addition to the one above, is that:

> Equal access to the job market for both sexes is desirable (regardless of qualifications).

This is a matter of opinion, not fact.

Sometimes assumptions are based on speculations about future events, and both the above statements fall into this category. They assume that because girls are doing better than boys in school now, they will continue to do so. The assumptions could be rephrased as **hypothetical reasoning**, based on the *if…then…* structure.

> If girls are doing well academically now, then they will continue to do well in the future (affecting the gender balance of the job market).

Since we can never predict the future with certainty, assumptions based on hypothetical reasoning are unsafe.

> **Exam tip**
>
> Assumptions may be assessed as **reasonable**, **sound**, **safe** or **justified**, or as **false** or **unjustified**, or it may be necessary to defer judgement until further information is available.

## Evaluating reasons

Revised ☐

Claims may be supported by reasons based on hard evidence, opinion, gossip or convincing examples and they should be assessed accordingly.

Reasons must provide **sufficient** support for the conclusion and so they need to be **adequate**.

> Cars should be banned because some people drive them dangerously, causing harm to others.

is an inadequately supported argument. The folly of 'some people' is insufficient grounds for banning the majority from an activity, unless the harm done vastly outweighs the benefits. At best, the reason supplied gives only **limited support** to the argument. The conclusion is **overdrawn** — too strong for the evidence. A weaker conclusion for which the reason might be seen as adequate is:

> People convicted of driving dangerously on several occasions pose a severe risk to the public, so they should be banned from driving.

**Adequate** means that words in the conclusion such as *always, all, no, never, definitely*, or the implication that this claim can be applied **universally**, are justified by the reason given. Here it would not be justifiable to ban *all* drivers, but it would be justifiable to ban those frequently convicted of dangerous driving.

The **significance** of a reason means how important it is relative to others.

> Sociology attracts far fewer students than psychology at our college. We should drop the sociology option for future years.

In a small school on a tight budget, a class of four sociologists might be considered unsustainable, but popularity might be viewed as less significant than meeting individual needs, especially if enough money were available for staff wages.

Reasons must also be **relevant**. Look at the following example:

> Children should not be asked to take home classroom pets to look after in the school holidays as rabies is a life-threatening disease.

> If reasons are not **adequate** and **relevant** or are insignificant and **selective**, then conclusions based on them may be **overdrawn**, unreasonable and implausible.

If the argument relates to British schools, it is highly unlikely that classroom pets would suffer from rabies. The reason might be more relevant in an overseas context.

Another aspect of poor reasoning is **selectivity**.

> Don't take your holidays in Brittany. Tripe sausages are their speciality.

is an example. Though andouillette (a coarse-grained tripe sausage) is served throughout Brittany, there are many alternative dishes, and the cuisine is only one of many factors to consider when choosing a holiday.

If an argument is based on reasons that are unconvincing for any of the reasons above, it is said not to be **reasonable** and any outcomes proposed in it may not be **plausible** (likely).

> **Exam tip**
>
> Ensure you memorise definitions of components and terms for assessing evidence such as **adequate** and **relevant** so that you do not confuse them.

## Evaluating evidence

Revised

Many arguments are based on evidence from research, which should be evaluated.

### Sample size

If only a small number of people were consulted about their experiences or views, this would produce insufficient data upon which to base conclusions. Evidence from a single institution, such as the results from one school, is too limited to produce a generalisation.

### Representativeness of sample

A sample might be large yet still not reflect the views of people from different backgrounds. To choose a representative sample, the researcher decides what attributes of potential interviewees might impact on their experience or opinions about the topic. These are often age, gender, social class and ethnicity, but other factors might be more crucial. In a survey of A-level students, the subjects they studied and whether they were members of year 12 or year 13 might be significant influences on their responses.

Once a detailed picture is obtained of the whole target population, the researcher chooses a representative sample of respondents reflecting all these different subgroups in the **correct proportions**. Volunteers, personal acquaintances (an opportunity sample) or people in the street are unlikely to be a representative sample.

> **Exam tip**
>
> Remember that large samples are not necessarily representative of the relevant population.

> **Now test yourself**
>
> 6 Would views collected from 1,000 readers of the *Daily Mirror* constitute a representative sample of British people?
>
> Tested

### How and when the evidence was collected

Research data being used to support a conclusion must be recent and relevant to the location, types of people and situation being discussed. Research into alcoholism in Glasgow might not necessarily be transferable enough to suggest ways of tackling the problem in England.

Sociologists and psychologists try to collect their data in carefully controlled conditions, seeking privacy for their interviewees and ensuring that they understand the questions. However, amateur researchers may try to interview people with others listening, making them less likely to tell the truth, or stop people in the street who have little time to answer properly and who lack interest. To be **valid**, data have to reflect a true picture of the situation being studied. This means that the respondent

> **Exam tip**
>
> Examine the source of any research data provided and try to make a reasoned judgement about how professional the body conducting it is likely to be.

> **Now test yourself**
>
> 7 What is meant by the terms 'representative sample' and 'valid data'?
>
> Tested

must fully understand the questions, take them seriously and be motivated to tell the truth.

## Ambiguity of findings

**Ambiguous** means having more than one possible meaning. A positive answer to the question:

> Do you often row with your family?

could reflect an enthusiasm for boating or an aggressive personality.

Research results are sometimes interpreted in a way that fits the expectation of the researcher. The small proportion of female MPs could be taken to suggest that women are not interested in politics, yet it might be that the long hours MPs spend away from home deter many potential women candidates.

## Alternative interpretations of statistics

Researchers rarely publish all the raw statistics they have collected, preferring to process them so that readers can understand the general trends.

- The **mode** is the most common score in a series. For example, in a test more students scored 11 out of 20 than any other number.
- The **mean** (average) mark could be considerably higher or lower if the majority of students scored a lot more or a lot less than 11.
- The **median** mark (the middle score of all of them) would probably be different again.
- Instead of using these **measures of central tendency**, an alternative way of representing the scores would be by the **range** — for example from 4 to 20 — but this reveals how only two of the students fared. Anyone wishing to present the class's efforts in a particularly positive or negative way might present their scores in the way most likely to produce the required impression. Researchers may do the same.

Journalists and advertisers may select particular statistics to support their argument, ignoring other available data that might have conveyed a different impression. Members of the government cite figures for decreases in certain types of crime while ignoring increases in other types, while the Opposition does the opposite. Phrases such as 'up to three quarters' can be misleading, since this is so vague it could refer to a very low proportion.

In the case of data based on interview questions, check exactly what was asked. The finding that only 3% of people who were asked where they would like to go on holiday chose France might give a negative impression, but if respondents were allowed to select only three options from a list of 50 countries, the result would be less surprising.

### Now test yourself

8 Explain the three measures of central tendency — mode, mean and median — in your own words. Suggest why on school reports teachers might prefer to compare individuals' test results with the class median rather than with the mean, mode or range of marks.

Answers on p. 102

Tested

### Exam tip

Distrust statistics preceded by phrases such as 'up to', 'nearly' and 'about'.

## Tips for evaluating reasoning

Revised

- Ensure that your answer is thorough enough, reflecting the space in the answer booklet and mark allocation.
- Make sure your response is as precisely worded as possible.
- Read each question twice to ensure that you have grasped the meaning.

### Typical mistakes

Candidates often answer too briefly. 'The sample size is large' merits only 1 mark because it is not fully explained. 'The sample size is large, which increases the chance of a wide variety of views being represented' could score 2 marks.

- Questions worth more than 3 marks need planning. These may ask you to state how far the reasons in a document support the conclusion, making two developed points. They could relate to the relevance or adequacy of the evidence or examples supporting the reasons. Your response should be paragraphed and detailed enough to fill most of the space provided, illustrated by references to the text. Spelling, grammar and punctuation need to be good.

**Exam tip**

Practise working in timed conditions.

**Exam tip**

If time is short, concentrate on the questions carrying the most marks, usually those at the end of the section or paper.

## Check your understanding

1 What is the difference between an argument and an explanation?

2 A counter-argument consists of which two parts?

3 Suggest two indicator words that flag up a conclusion.

4 How can we distinguish evidence from examples?

5 What is another word for a component of argument?

6 Suggest two things you should not do when asked to identify a component such as the conclusion from a document.

7 What is meant by an assumption in critical thinking?

8 Why are there no argument indicators for assumptions?

9 Explain the meaning of hypothetical reasoning.

10 Suggest three ways in which reasons might fail to support a conclusion.

Answers on p. 102

## Exam practice

Read the following passage and answer the questions that follow:

**Paid work disadvantages students**

**Schools and colleges selecting applicants for A-level courses should discriminate against those who insist on doing part-time work. This has a negative effect on their academic results.**

**It may be argued that the experience of paid work enhances students' chances of obtaining full-time work later, but the type of part-time work A-level students do is generally unskilled, quite unlike their career aspirations. Obtaining good A-levels is far more important for professional careers.**

**Teachers are fully aware that the students who perform best in their A-levels tend to be those without part-time jobs. Now a study by the Economic and Social Research Institute in Dublin has proved the connection. In a survey of one-sixth of Irish secondary schools in 2007, they found that working part-time at upper secondary level was associated with underperformance and also led to increased dropout.**

**Earning money not only takes up time that could be devoted to study but tempts students to waste more time spending their earnings. Sixth-form tutor Win Roberts of Bright's Comprehensive School in Reading said, 'I've noticed many times that it's the girls who work on Saturdays who spend their study periods looking through magazines to decide what to buy with their earnings.'**

**A** Identify the main conclusion of the passage. [3]

**B** State the counter-assertion. [3]

**C** An example is given in the final paragraph. Explain one way in which this example may or may not be representative. [2]

**D** Assess how strongly the reasons and evidence presented support the conclusion. You should include two developed points, referring directly to the links between the reasons and evidence and the conclusion. [6]

**Answers online**

Online

## Exam summary

✔ The section on language of reasoning primarily tests your skills of analysis (AO1) and evaluation (AO2), although quality of communication (AO3) is always assessed.

✔ Unit 1 comprises 50% of the total AS mark. This section is usually worth 35 marks out of a total 75 marks for Unit 1.

✔ You should be able to identify an argument (as opposed to an explanation, claim or assertion, for example) and recognise that it has a structure with reasons and a conclusion linked together. Recognising argument indicators will help with this analysis. The early questions on the paper will ask you to identify some of the following components or elements in particular paragraphs of the documents:

- conclusion
- reasons
- argument indicators
- assertions or claims
- counter-assertions or counter-claims
- counter-arguments, including counter-conclusion and counter-reason
- evidence
- examples
- explanation
- simple hypothetical reasoning, which takes the common 'if this, then that' form
- assumptions, including instances where an argument requires more than one assumption

✔ When asked to identify such components, quote the author's words exactly unless:

- you need to substitute a noun for a pronoun to make the meaning clearer
- the component has another one, such as an example, embedded within it

✔ Avoid ellipses (substituting dots for words to save time when quoting).

✔ If a particular sentence or phrase from the passage is quoted, you will be required to identify what component it is (e.g. a counter-assertion) and explain your answer.

✔ You will be required to assess the claims made in the passage provided by commenting on:

- the type of reasoning involved; for example, whether it is hypothetical or based on sound evidence
- the size of any survey sample quoted
- the representative nature of the sample
- how and when the evidence was collected
- the potential ambiguity of any findings
- alternative interpretations of any statistics

✔ In addition you may need to:

- state assumptions that must be made in order to support a claim
- supply a reason of your own to support a claim
- assess how far the reasons support the conclusion, making several developed points that refer directly to the links between them. For this task, good planning, organisation and expression are essential.

# 2 Credibility

In this part of the examination you will encounter one or more documents presenting contrasting claims — different points of view about a particular scenario, or different accounts of an event. You will need to identify, assess and compare the claims by considering their credibility and the reasoning that supports or undermines them. This may include making an assessment of whether visual material, such as photographs or graphs, or other evidence, really supports the claims it accompanies. The outcomes predicted by some sources may strike you as **implausible** (unlikely) because they are based on weak reasoning and evidence.

However, most of your judgements will be reached by applying **credibility criteria**, the names and meanings of which you must learn as they will not be provided on the examination paper.

> A **plausible claim** is likely and reasonable because it is supported by sound reasoning and evidence.

> **Credible** means believable. A **criterion** is a standard, rule, or test on which a judgement or decision can be based; the plural form is criteria.

## Credibility criteria

### Corroboration or consistency
Revised

We are more likely to believe a witness if another person corroborates his or her account or if the account is both internally consistent and consistent with other sources. Where there is conflict between or within accounts, credibility is reduced.

### Reputation
Revised

Reputation may relate to facts about the character of particular individuals mentioned in the text, such as a police record. If no such information is provided, you can conjecture how reputable those making claims may be on the basis of their professions or similar attributes, even though this sounds like stereotyping. Clergy, doctors, police and lawyers are expected to be honest so we could expect them to be able to give honest accounts of events. Professionals have to consider their public reputations, so it would be unwise for them to lie.

The BBC, quality national newspapers such as *The Times* and *Guardian*, and government websites have a better reputation for reliability than amateur websites.

## Ability to see or perceive

Consider whether eyewitnesses were able to see well, considering factors such as distance, weather conditions, distractions, obstacles and time of day. CCTV evidence may be indistinct and photographs may have been manipulated, as may sound recordings.

Think whether the media reporter was an eyewitness and therefore a **primary source**, or whether the information was bought from a news agency (a **secondary source**), or from an interviewee closely involved in the incident. Did the interviewee see events at first hand, or hear about them from others, depending on hearsay?

> People or organisations making claims are referred to as **sources**.
>
> A **primary source** has found out about a phenomenon at first hand using a primary method, such as an experiment, survey or observation. A **secondary source** is a pre-existing one, for example a published account of a discovery, which you might read and summarise as part of an essay.

## Vested interest

Consider whether a witness or interviewee would personally gain from making a false, biased or selective claim by winning a court case and gaining compensation or avoiding loss of reputation. In the case of media sources, concerns about national security, election success or attracting more readers may influence the slant of a story. On the other hand, professionals may have vested interests in presenting accurate and unbiased accounts to preserve their reputations.

## Expertise or experience

Think about whether witnesses or interviewees have relevant knowledge and experience to give sound evidence. Even experts in one field may know insufficient about the precise topic in question.

## Neutrality

Lack of neutrality means that an individual is likely to favour a particular position or party because of emotional ties. Objectivity is lost because of friendships, family relationships, nationality, religion and other affiliations.

In the case of a news medium, consider whether it has right- or left-wing **bias**, which country it is written in or what other interests it may reflect. Neutral sources are likely to present evidence and views from conflicting sides and the BBC always tries to do this, even though some people argue that it has a moderate agenda, avoiding interviewing extremists of all types.

> **Exam tip**
>
> Note the difference between bias or lack of neutrality, and vested interest. People lacking neutrality may not tell the whole truth because of fellow feeling for others involved. Those with vested interests might lie for personal gain or to avoid harm to themselves.

## Now test yourself

1 Designer John Galliano was sacked from Christian Dior in 2011 for allegedly hurling anti-Semitic insults at an art historian in a bar. He denied it. Later a video clip emerged showing Galliano in a separate incident in the same bar telling two customers that their parents should have been gassed.

Identify two credibility criteria that you would apply to decide whether he was likely to be guilty of insulting the art historian, and explain your answer.

## Applying the credibility criteria

You will be asked to assess the credibility of particular individuals or organisations by identifying and applying appropriate criteria, supporting this with reference to the text.

- Use the established terms above for the criteria, not phrases of your own. For example, write 'expertise' rather than 'specialist knowledge'.
- Explain how the criterion is relevant. For example, show how you know the source has expertise by referring to, or quoting from, the text.
- Use the phrase 'weakens credibility' or 'strengthens credibility', being explicit about whether the criterion makes the source more or less believable.

> **Exam tip**
>
> The credibility criteria are easily identified by their initial letters, CRAVEN.

> **Exam tip**
>
> Ensure that you quote from documents to support your answer and identify the sources of quotations.

## Now test yourself

2  Recall the criteria indicated by the mnemonic CRAVEN and explain the meaning of each one.

Answers on p. 102

# Assessment of visual material

Documents may be accompanied by photographs, graphs or artists' impressions of events, with questions asking you to assess the degree to which these images or their accompanying captions support the claims being made.

You could be asked to assess the support given by a photograph to its caption.

## Assessing a photograph or image

Ask yourself the following questions about photographs or images you have to assess:

- Could the photograph have been faked, manipulated or cropped to suggest an event that did not really happen or to create a misleading impression?
- Look at the background of a photograph to see if it enables you to judge the scale of the crucial objects.
- How certain can you be that this photograph is a typical example of what is being described and not a 'worst case scenario' or a site specially prepared for the photograph?
- Is the photograph too blurred or too small for you to be certain what is being shown?
- Could the camera angle or lighting be contrived to make the people or situation look particularly threatening? For example, photographs taken from below speakers or in front of oncoming marchers or police can make their looming shapes quite alarming.

- Does the object that has been photographed look like the genuine article, or could it be a replica?
- Was the artist's impression of the scene produced by an eyewitness?
- Scrutinise the captions accompanying illustrations. In newspapers there is a tendency for the caption to convey a simpler message than the article itself.
- Does the accompanying caption convey exactly what is shown in the photograph and relate precisely to the claims in the passage, or are there minor but significant differences between them?
- In the case of graphs, check precisely what is being measured for relevance.

# Tackling other types of questions

Other types of questions you may encounter in this section of Unit 1 are discussed below.

## What else would you need to know? ———————————— Revised ☐

**Explain what other information you would need to know in order to reach one of your points of assessment about the credibility of a named source.**

The answer will obviously depend on what information is missing from the document, but some possibilities are that we would need to know whether the person or source:

- represents the views of many or is expressing a personal opinion
- was an eyewitness or is relying on someone else's account (ability to see)
- is likely to be rewarded in some way for making the claim (vested interest)
- is an expert in the specific field in question (relevant expertise)
- has close relationships with those whose views or interest the claim is supporting (lack of neutrality)

Your answer needs to clarify the possible effects on the person's credibility if these facts were known.

A variation on this question, requiring the negative equivalent of the answers above, might ask what you would need to assume in order to believe the person's claim.

## Questions about consistency ———————————————— Revised ☐

**Identify one source and their claim that would be *consistent* with this claim.**

This entails simply copying out a claim that supports the statement provided and stating who makes it and in which document. Do not reword the claim or offer an explanation.

Follow the same advice for the companion question:

**Identify two claims and their sources that would be *inconsistent* with this claim.**

Copy out claims that contradict the statement provided, stating who made them and in which document.

**Exam tip**

Always read questions carefully. It is easy to lose marks for simple omissions, such as not mentioning the source of a claim.

## Longer questions

Revised

**Write a reasoned case coming to a judgement about the scheme discussed in the documents. You should assess:**
- **the relative credibility of the two sides**
- **the relative plausibility (likelihood) of the scheme being successful**

**Your answers should contain sustained comparisons within each of these tasks and must refer to the material in the documents.**

**Exam tip**

Answer in the appropriate amount of detail to fit the marks available, explaining your answer where necessary.

As the final question on the paper, this may carry about 16 marks and needs careful planning. Assume that the two parts are about equally weighted, so write similar amounts, in separate paragraphs.

For the relative credibility section:
- Make notes, organising those who are making claims into two groups, regardless of whether they are individuals or organisations.
- Jot down which credibility criteria strengthen or weaken each side.
- Aim for a well organised answer, identifying criteria that apply to several members of a particular side as opposed to making random assessments of each individual.
- Provide a balanced assessment of each side, comparing them by using phrases such as 'there is vested interest on both sides…', but then suggest criteria that you consider to be the most significant in this scenario, tipping the balance.
- You may argue for either side being more credible as long as this is consistent with your reasoning.

To discuss relative plausibility:
- Make notes about the strengths and weaknesses of the reasons, evidence and examples provided by each side, or highlight the documents accordingly. Assess factors such as the following:
  - whether reasoning fails to support the conclusions by being hypothetical, inadequate, irrelevant, selective or based on unsafe assumptions
  - whether evidence is based on convincing, representative research or biased opinion
  - whether examples are relevant to the current situation
  - the extent to which there is corroboration (agreement) or contradiction between sources

- Discuss the plausibility of one side at a time, presenting a balanced view of each.
- Compare them and then identify which strengths or weaknesses are important enough to make one seem more likely or reasonable.
- Finally, write a sentence or two reaching an overall judgement as to which side is the more convincing, taking both credibility and plausibility into account.

### Typical mistakes

Candidates sometimes fail to distinguish credibility (whether sources are believable) from plausibility (whether reasoning and evidence are reasonable and convincing). They should be discussed in separate paragraphs.

## Check your understanding

Tested

1 What exactly is meant by a credibility criterion?
2 How does vested interest differ from bias?
3 Why is the term 'ability to perceive' sometimes preferred to 'ability to see'?
4 What is meant by hearsay?
5 What is meant by plausibility?

Answers on p. 103

## Exam practice

Read the passages below and then answer the question that follows:

**Document 1: Quick fixes seldom lead to long-term change**

**There's little evidence that people stick with any miracle diet over the long-term. Too often, diets fail to give people the tools needed for coping with common dilemmas.**

**'At first a diet stimulates interest because you're doing something different,' says Jennifer K. Nelson, M.S., R.D., a clinical dietician at Mayo Clinic, Rochester, Minn. 'But in the long run, you've still got to face that when you go to mom's for home-made ice cream, or that vacation when you're on the road and you stop at a fast-food place. Then the diet becomes a ball and chain. The best program equips you to deal with these common situations,' says Nelson.**

**'On high protein diets people can temporarily lose large amounts of weight, and can even lower their blood cholesterol, sugar, and triglycerides,' says John McDougall, M.D., 'but the method is unhealthy.' ...**

**[These diets] contain significant amounts of the very foods — the meats — that the American Cancer Society and the Heart Association tell us contribute to our most common causes of death and disability. There is a simpler, healthier answer to obesity: eat the foods that thin people around the world eat; for example, the healthy people of Asia who thrive on high-complex-carbohydrate, high-vegetable, rice-based diets.**

(Extract from 'High-Protein "Miracle" Diets', an article on the VegSource website)

**Document 2: The 10 kg in 10 Day Program Can Work — For You!**

**Hi! I'm Fred Jones and I lost 10 kilos in 10 days. You can do it too.**

**I needed to lose weight fast to pass my next fitness test as a fireman so I had to devise a diet plan that enabled me to lose 10 kilos easily, healthily and permanently.**

**My method is a simple program which includes ordinary foods but in particular combinations for 10 days. It has already helped thousands of people lose 10 kilos or more in as little as 10 days. Before you waste your money on another diet program, look at these success stories:**

**'Fred, thank you so much for the easy step by step diet. I had doubts but decided to give it a try. It's my 5th day and I've already lost over 5 kilos! I will let you know my weight loss after 10 days.' Janice, Brighton**

**'Hi Fred, it's been 2 weeks since I finished the diet. I'm amazed that all the weight is still off, your post diet ideas are terrific!! I feel like a new person, almost 12 kilos lighter thanks to you!!' Gill, Manchester**

**'Thanks for the miracle. I have been dieting on and off for most of my life and I have never been as pleased as this before. I'm now only 60 kilos and couldn't have done it without your diet.' Harriet, Aberdeen**

**Try the 10 in 10 plan now. I'll show you how to do it day by day, meal by meal and if you don't lose any weight within the first 10 days of my special diet I'll refund your money.**

**For my amazing plan send only £20 to the above address. Limited time discount offer.**

(Source: internet website)

Write a reasoned case, coming to a judgement about quick weight loss diets. You should assess:

● the relative credibility of the two sides
● the relative plausibility (likelihood) of quick weight loss diets being successful

Your answer should contain sustained comparisons within each of these tasks and must refer to the material in the documents.

[16]

**Answers and Unit 1 quick quiz online**

Online

## Exam summary

✔ The credibility section primarily tests your skills of evaluation (AO2), although in order to assess the material you will need to recognise any components of argument, such as assumptions, mentioned in the questions (AO1). Quality of communication (AO3) is always assessed.

✔ This section is usually worth 40 marks out of a total 75 marks for Unit 1.

✔ You should be able to identify and assess different claims by considering the credibility of sources using the CRAVEN criteria. Explain how claims are strengthened or weakened by circumstantial evidence or aspects of the context and the following attributes of the sources:

● reputation
● ability to see or perceive
● vested interest
● expertise or experience
● neutrality

✔ You should be able to assess the extent to which visual material supports a claim.

✔ For assessing plausibility, use your skills from the first section to assess whether:

● reasons and evidence are adequate, relevant and significant enough to support the conclusions reached

● statistics and other research data could be misleading

● reasoning is based on hypothetical reasoning or unjustified assumptions

✔ Your answers must contain sustained comparisons within each of these tasks and refer to the material within the documents.

✔ Consider the strengths and weaknesses of both sides and then decide which are most significant and make an overall judgement.

✔ You should also be able to:

● identify and explain what other information would be needed in order to reach a judgement about the credibility of a particular document or source

● identify a claim and its source, within a particular document, that is consistent or inconsistent with a given claim

✔ Learn the credibility criteria, ensuring that you do not confuse vested interest with lack of neutrality.

# 3 Analysis of argument

In Unit 2, unlike Unit 1, it is impractical to revise for each section of the paper separately because section A (the multiple choice paper) and section B require the same skills of analysis and evaluation. Section C is quite different, requiring you to develop your own arguments.

# Further elements of argument

In addition to the components or elements of argument covered in Unit 1, in sections A and B of the Unit 2 paper you need to be able to recognise the following and in section B explain their role in the structure of the argument provided.

## Intermediate conclusion — Revised ☐

While a short argument may consist only of a couple of reasons supporting a single conclusion, longer arguments often consist of groups of reasons supported by evidence and examples. Each of these leads to a preliminary conclusion, known as an **intermediate conclusion**. This may be the case when you write an essay. Each paragraph or section may end with a sentence such as 'This shows that', or may begin with a general statement that is then supported by the rest of the paragraph. These concluding or opening sentences may be intermediate conclusions. The main or overall conclusion of your essay, which is likely to be in the last paragraph, is supported by these intermediate conclusions.

> An **intermediate conclusion** is a conclusion drawn on the way to the main conclusion, supported by reasons but acting itself as a reason for the main conclusion or other intermediate conclusions.

In the hierarchy of a complex argument, intermediate conclusions function both as conclusions to groups of reasons and the evidence supporting them, and as reasons supporting the main conclusion.

Even in a relatively short argument, you may find an intermediate conclusion preceding the final one.

> **You have a massive file of notes (R), so it will take you a long time to read through them all and digest the content (IC). You need to begin your revision early (C).**

The component 'so it will take you a long time to read through them all and digest the content' forms a step in the line of reasoning between the reason (R) 'You have a massive file of notes' and the main conclusion, the second sentence. The indicator word 'so' provides a clue that it is some kind of conclusion.

In the first part of the Unit 2 paper, it is important to be able to distinguish intermediate conclusions from conclusions. Several of the multiple-choice questions may ask you to identify either an intermediate conclusion or a main conclusion from a range of options. Some of the distracters (wrong options) for a conclusion question are likely to be intermediate conclusions and vice versa.

Likewise you will need to be able to distinguish the two in analysis questions in this unit. Remember that the order of an argument on the page does not necessarily reflect the order of the reasoning. Just as a conclusion may precede a reason, a conclusion may precede an intermediate conclusion. It is quite common in a long passage for the conclusion to be the first sentence and the intermediate conclusion to be the last.

**Exam tip**

If you cannot distinguish the intermediate from the main conclusion, try the 'therefore' test. Say both statements with 'therefore' in between them and then reverse them and try it again. This will help you see which follows logically from the other.

## Now test yourself

Tested

1  Analyse the following argument, identifying all elements, including the intermediate conclusion.

**People who are very similar tend to be attracted to each other. However, when we know someone is a relative our strong incest taboo normally makes us resist any attraction to him or her. It is therefore important that people know who their close relatives are. Occasionally siblings are brought up apart without knowing who their biological parents are, as in the recent case of the twins parted at birth who married each other and later found out their true identities. People who adopt children must ensure that they are informed about their biological parents as early as possible.**

## Analogy

Revised

An **analogy** is a comparison used as part of the reasoning in an argument. The writer may try to persuade you that the situation in question is similar to a less controversial one, so what is almost certainly true for a familiar situation must therefore be true for the apparently similar issue in question. Here is an example:

> **The Yorkshire Ripper is making a legal bid for freedom by claiming his human rights have been breached. Peter Sutcliffe, who was jailed in 1981 for murdering 13 women, will argue that the Home Office disregarded his human rights because it failed to fix a tariff for his sentence. Harry Smelt, whose wife, Olive, survived an attack by Sutcliffe, said 'He didn't give the victims many human rights, did he?'**

(Adapted from *Metro*, 15 May 2008)

In the above passage, the conclusion to Harry Smelt's argument is implied rather than stated, but he is making an analogy between Sutcliffe's treatment of his victims and how the criminal justice system should treat him. His suggestion seems to be that, as the Ripper accorded his victims few human rights, he should receive few and therefore should not be freed.

Exam questions about analogies usually require both analysis and assessment. You may be asked:

● to identify the analogy in a particular paragraph by copying it out

● to explain what is being compared

● to assess how well the analogy supports the author's argument

This last type of question requires evaluation skills, which are discussed on pages 32–45.

Explaining what is being compared in an analogy requires some precision. Candidates lose marks by responses that are too brief or vague. In the example above, stating that the Ripper was being compared with his victims might not be accurate enough to earn full marks. It is more precise to say that the Ripper's entitlement to human rights is being compared to his victims' human rights entitlement.

## General principles

Revised

**General principles** are 'rule-like' statements or guidelines about behaviour that is not limited to a specific situation. Principles sometimes act as reasons to support arguments, although they can be found in other contexts, such as the mission statements of organisations. Two examples are:

> We must seek to preserve the natural world.

> Adults should never put their own needs before those of their children.

> **A general principle** outlines desirable behaviour or priorities that should apply in a broad range of situations.

Many such principles are ethical principles, making universal statements about how people should or should not behave or what our values or priorities should be. They are expressions of opinion rather than claims about which absolutely everyone would agree. In some contexts, principles are underlying assumptions in an argument rather than being explicitly stated.

In Unit 2, you could be asked to:
- identify the best statement of a general principle being used in a short passage from a series of options in the multiple-choice section
- identify a general principle in an argument
- evaluate how consistently a principle is applied as part of the evaluation of reasoning

In the section on developing your own arguments, you could be asked to construct an argument on a given topic:
- including a principle as a reason
- supporting or challenging a principle supplied

During the popular uprising in Libya in 2011, the United Nations adopted the principle that 'we have a duty to protect civilians of any nation from aggression'.

> **Exam tip**
>
> Remember that a general principle must apply to a broad range of situations, not just to a specific one.

Notice that principles are quite broad. 'We have a duty to protect civilians in Libya from attacks by Gaddafi's forces' is not a general principle because it applies to only one specific situation, whereas 'Other countries should not interfere in the affairs of a sovereign nation' is a general principle.

Principles often begin with phrases such as:

> Society must...
>
> People ought not to...
>
> It is wrong to...

or make use of a passive construction such as:

> The needs of X must be given priority.

## Now test yourself

2  Examine the letter below written by two readers to a national newspaper in July 2007 and answer the questions that follow. To help you understand the comment, 'internment' means imprisonment without trial, a situation in which the state makes no formal charges against which prisoners can defend themselves. This relates to the imprisonment of terrorist suspects while evidence is sought against them.

**It's always been our understanding that in a liberal democracy the role of the police was to protect our freedoms. When did those hard-won principles become inverted so that the overriding concern becomes disproportionate police powers — i.e. proposals to introduce internment? When did the terrorists win?**

a  Identify the principle the letter writers associate with a liberal democracy and why they think it has been 'inverted'.

b  Suggest how a counter-argument could reason that internment is upholding one of the principles of a liberal democracy.

## Distinguishing explanations from arguments

The difference between explanations and arguments is discussed in Unit 1 (see page 8). In Unit 2 you are expected to be able to distinguish between them, for example in the multiple-choice test. Remember that an argument must attempt to persuade, to change behaviour, beliefs or attitudes, as opposed to simply informing. An argument must have reasons and a conclusion, and the conclusion must follow from the reasons. A collection of pieces of evidence or reasons together with a conclusion that is not clearly connected is not an argument.

## Key terminology

You should be able to understand and use the following terms accurately, according to their meaning in critical thinking.

### Counter

As a verb, this means to oppose an argument, usually by providing reasoning against it. It is used as a prefix in words such as 'counter-argument', 'counter-assertion', 'counter-claim' and 'counter-example' (one that suggests an exception to evidence amassed to support the main argument).

### Challenge

As a verb, this means the same as to counter an argument. In Unit 2 you will be asked to write an argument either supporting (giving reasons and evidence in line with) or challenging the main conclusion in the document. Challenge is also used as a noun. A counter-argument or counter-claim is often followed by a particular kind of reason known as a challenge or response to the counter-argument. For example:

> Although some people think A-levels have become easier over the years (counter-claim), they are mistaken (challenge or response to the counter-claim). Examinations have in fact become much harder (conclusion). This is because...

(Reasons and evidence would follow.)

## Assess

This synonym for 'evaluate' usually invites you to consider an example of reasoning and to identify strengths and/or weaknesses, supported by explanation and, if appropriate, quotation. In such a case, make a conscious effort to consider strengths, as the emphasis of your course may have been more on flaws.

## Strength and weakness

At other times, questions may specifically direct you to identify and explain only strengths in reasoning, such as adequacy and relevance. Alternatively they may ask you to identify a number of weaknesses, to name the flaws and to explain why they are examples of poor reasoning.

## Opinion, belief and knowledge

These familiar words are included in the list to enable you to distinguish between different types of evidence. An opinion is **subjective** (a personal view) and is therefore not such reliable evidence as knowledge, which is universally accepted as **objective** (neutral or unbiased) fact. The word 'belief' carries the possibility of error. Many beliefs are shared by large numbers of people on the basis of substantial evidence, but individuals may hold other beliefs on the basis of faith or complete misunderstandings. If a belief is stated, it can be called a claim.

> **Subjective** evidence is opinion-based whereas **objective** data are not influenced by personal bias.

## Reasoning

This refers to a coherent and logical pattern of thought leading from one step to another, usually employing reasons, evidence, intermediate conclusions and other components, to reach a conclusion. As well as in arguments, reasoning is employed in explanations and in tentative academic explorations of ideas such as theories and hypotheses. The word is sometimes used in a looser way to refer to the way a writer has attempted to persuade in a long passage that may include emotional appeals and flaws; poor reasoning in fact.

## Coherent

A coherent argument is a meaningful and well-reasoned one where the steps flow logically from each other and all points are relevant.

## Consistent

A consistent argument is one without internal contradictions. All the evidence and reasoning corroborates or supports it.

## Contradiction

Contradiction, or conflict, occurs when two or more claims undermine each other, showing that at least one cannot be completely true.

## Converse

The converse of a statement is one where the key sections, such as subject and direct object, have been reversed. The converse of 'Drug addiction increases unemployment' is 'Unemployment increases drug addiction'.

Note that the word converse means 'the other way round', not 'the opposite' (which would be 'Drug addiction does not increase unemployment').

## Refute

Refute means to prove a claim wrong.

## Repudiate

Repudiate means emphatically to reject an argument or idea. This could be by employing good reasoning or by offering poor reasoning or no reasoning at all, by ranting. This contrasts with refuting a claim, where the reasoning has definitely been successful in dismissing it.

## Structure

The structure of the argument refers to its various components or elements and the order and way in which they function to support its conclusion.

## Draw a conclusion

Multiple-choice questions will sometimes invite you to identify the best statement of the conclusion you would draw from a list of options relating to the reasoning presented in a short passage. In such a case you would need to work through the reasoning and choose a conclusion that is broad enough to flow from all the reasons and yet not overdrawn. Ensure that it represents the final stage in the reasoning and is therefore the overall conclusion, not an intermediate one.

> **Exam tip**
>
> Remember that an overdrawn conclusion is based on inadequate reasoning. The available reasons and evidence support a more limited conclusion.

## Inference

An inference is something a reader, listener or observer infers or works out from the evidence or clues in a text, in the spoken word or similar stimulus. As the point inferred is not made explicitly (directly and openly), there is always a chance that the reader may interpret the evidence wrongly, inferring something that is not true.

## Implication

A word that is often confused with inference is 'implication'. This refers to the indirect suggestion that something may be the case, as opposed to explicitly (directly) stating that it is.

It is quite common to find examination questions such as:

> What is the arguer inferring from the evidence he has quoted in paragraph 2? What alternative explanation could there be for the phenomenon he observed?

or

> What may the passage imply is the reason for...?

> **Typical mistakes**
>
> People often confuse the words 'imply' and 'infer'. Remember that a passage or speaker implies or suggests something, whereas the reader or listener infers the implicit meaning.

## Ambiguity

Ambiguous statements can be interpreted in different ways because of double or even multiple possible meanings. Examination questions may ask you to assess evidence that could be ambiguous. For example, '75% of NUT members expressed no wish to go on strike' could mean that:

- 75% of those balloted by the NUT voted no to going on strike
- 75% of those balloted by the NUT either voted no or abstained
- 75% of all NUT members did not express support for the strike; many of them did not participate in a ballot at all so their views are unknown

You should be able to see that the first option gives a much stronger impression of opposition to strike action than the other two.

Many abstract words can be interpreted in different ways, e.g. an attempt to achieve 'equality' could mean giving everyone the same or giving poorer people more to close the gap between them and the wealthy.

Multiple-choice questions may ask you to select the closest definition of an ambiguous word or phrase as it is used in the passage.

## Now test yourself

Tested ☐

3 Read the paragraph below:

**Doubts about the good sense of the British justice system have recently been raised. Sarah Davies (20) was awarded a £75 fine for littering when she offered a small piece of sausage roll to her daughter in a park and the child dropped it on the ground. Gareth Corkhill was fined £210 for overfilling his wheelie bin so the lid was raised a few inches. When others receive only cautions for vandalism and theft, can this really be justice?**

(Facts from the *Daily Mail*, 25 April 2008)

Which of the following is the closest in meaning to the word 'justice' as used in the final sentence?

● the treatment of others in a fair and equitable manner

● the administration of law with the objectives of protecting victims and lawfully punishing perpetrators

Answers on p. 103

## Check your understanding

Tested ☐

1 Define an intermediate conclusion.

2 Rewrite the following ambiguous statement in two different ways to convey different meanings:
'She gave the persistent tramp a couple of socks to make him go away.'

Answers on p. 103

## Exam practice

Look at the following options and decide which one is an argument. [1]

**a** The washing machine is making a bleeping sound, so that indicates that it will be safe to open it.

**b** Research suggests that boys are reluctant readers whereas most girls enjoy it. Boys also find it harder to sit still for long. The sexes need to be taught in different ways.

**c** Gerbils are small rodents, which originally come from desert areas. There are about 110 different species. You should definitely choose gerbils as pets for your children.

**d** AS levels were developed in 2000, partly to provide qualifications for students who started life in the sixth form but then decided to terminate their studies after one year. In addition, studying more than three subjects provides a broader academic experience than formerly.

**Answers online**

 Online ☐

## Exam summary

✔ Unit 2 is worth 50% of the total AS marks.

✔ Section A of the Unit 2 paper consists of a number of short passages, and graphs, charts or diagrams, followed by multiple-choice questions with four options. Some of the source materials generate more than one set of questions. Section A is worth 15 marks maximum.

✔ Answer the questions by marking in pencil the appropriate letter on a sheet that can be scanned by an optical mark reader.

✔ The questions test your ability to analyse the structure of arguments (AO1) and to assess reasoning (AO2).

✔ To prepare, brush up your skills in the following:

- Distinguishing an argument from other material such as explanations, rants or collections of facts. An argument is a coherent attempt to persuade, with a conclusion supported by at least one relevant reason.

- Deciding which is the best statement of the main conclusion of the passage. This often means distinguishing it from intermediate conclusions and inaccurate conclusions.

- Deciding which of a number of options best supports or most weakens the argument in the passage.

- Deciding which statement is an underlying assumption or principle.

- Identifying the best statement of the intermediate conclusion or counter-assertion in the passage. This involves analysing the passage to identify the named component and then choosing the option exactly the same in meaning.

- Deciding which option is closest to the meaning of a particular word as used in the passage. This tests your awareness of ambiguity.

- Scrutinising a graph or chart and answering questions about which option could be an explanation for the results or reliably inferred from the data.

- Choosing which one of four lists or diagrams of components (making use of notations such as R1, C, Ev and CA) accurately conveys a brief argument's structure.

✔ To tackle multiple-choice questions:

- Look at the question first before reading the passage to focus your mind on what you are looking for.

- Then read the passage and decide what you think the answer is before reading the options, to avoid being distracted by wrong ones.

- Then read the options and choose the one nearest to your expectation.

- The process of elimination approach is recommended only if you have little idea about what the answer could be.

- There is often one answer that is the opposite of the correct one, one that is irrelevant and two that are very similar, one of which is the 'best statement' of the answer. Identify the exact difference in meaning between the options to select the correct one.

- If you really cannot decide, choose one of the better options randomly and move on, as you need to spend not much more than 1 minute per question in order to leave adequate time for sections B and C.

# 4 Evaluating arguments

## Flaws

Brush up on your analysis of the strengths and weaknesses of types of evidence, including statistics, from Unit 1. In addition, learn the names of the following flaws, getting as much practice as possible in recognising them in context. Ensure that you can explain *why* they constitute poor reasoning.

### Slippery slope or thin end of the wedge — Revised

Slippery slope or thin end of the wedge is a misleading chain of argument. It usually involves describing a situation that is supposedly deteriorating or which will deteriorate in an alarming manner if the first stage is allowed to occur. The flaw lies in the fact that, at one or more links in the chain, the arguer makes a generalisation that may not be justified. He or she predicts that something negative is bound to happen when it might not, or that the trend will affect huge numbers of people when it might affect only a few.

### Now test yourself — Tested

1　Spot the weak links in this slippery slope argument.

**Students should avoid taking out a loan if they go to university. The loaned money gives them a false sense of being well off, tempting them to spend the full amount of each year's loan on unnecessary luxuries. Then at the end of the course when they are unable to get a job straightaway, they have to start paying interest on the loan. As each year passes, the amount owed increases and so does the interest, making paying it off increasingly impossible. Mortgage lenders and others are reluctant to lend more money to the indebted, meaning ex-students can never have a home of their own. Discovering this breeds hopelessness, relationship break-up and depression, often leading to suicide.**

### Unjustified projection — Revised

Media sources often alarm the public by projecting current trends into the future. For example, a claim might be made that a rise in a particular type of crime or harmful activity, such as binge drinking over the past 5 years, might continue at an equally steep rate over the next few decades, eventually resulting in a huge epidemic. This is similar to a slippery slope argument but without necessarily having a chain of argument with tenuous links. Instead the error lies in taking for granted that the trend will continue at the current rate. More often steps are taken to reduce dangerous developments. Remember that the phrase 'if trends continue' heralds a hypothetical argument based on guesswork only.

## Post hoc argument

The Latin phrase post hoc means 'after this'. It refers to the assumption that, if an event follows 'after this', it was caused by this. For example, if a school's examination results in critical thinking improved after a particular critical thinking teacher had left, enemies of that teacher might be keen to suggest a link. However, it could be that results improved because the new specification was clearer, or more recent cohorts of students happened to be more motivated.

## Circular argument

A circular argument is one that appears at first to offer useful new information but nothing new is really established. This flaw in reasoning is also known as 'begging the question' because, despite appearances, it avoids the question rather than addressing it. Here is an example:

> Acts of crime and deviance occur most often in areas known as zones of transition. If you are trying to identify zones of transition in your town, you can easily recognise them by the high amounts of crime and deviance that occur there.

In this case, the first sentence appears to be about to offer an explanation of crime but then the reader is let down by being offered a definition of zones of transition, which simply loops back to the contents of the first sentence.

A more frequently cited example is when you are asked to accept a religious teaching because it is in some holy book. On querying the truth of the holy book, you are told to believe it because it is the words of a particular god or prophet. However, the only evidence for the existence of the god or prophet lies in the book itself.

## False dichotomy or restricting the options

A dichotomy refers to two possibilities. This type of reasoning puts forward a limited number of possibilities, usually two, from which the listener is invited to choose. Sometimes one is made to seem particularly unattractive as the other is the option the arguer wishes the listener to choose. If the listener does not think clearly enough to realise that other possibilities exist, he or she may be misled into choosing the least unattractive of those offered.

> Doctor to sick child: Would you like the injection in your arm or your bottom?
>
> Child: I'd rather not have it anywhere.

In this example, the precocious child has noticed that the options are restricted more than they need be.

A more cynical approach may be employed by advertisers:

> Do you want to risk your family facing disaster if your house is destroyed by flood or fire?
>
> Ask for details of our insurance policies today.

## Conflation, arguing from one thing to another and unrelated conclusion

Conflation refers to confusion over terms, specifically referring to two slightly different concepts as if they were exactly the same, such as 'poverty' and 'deprivation', or 'intelligence' and 'ability'. The terms are used interchangeably in the muddled thoughts of the arguer, or have been deliberately confused to mislead the reader. Look out for passages where evidence based on one concept sounds quite convincing and then this is supposedly backed up by evidence related to another, slightly different, concept. The conclusion is then presented, referring to only one of the concepts or perhaps to yet another concept not quite the same as either. This is poor reasoning because the evidence relating to some of the concepts was not as relevant as the argument implies. The conclusion reached is not supported by all the reasons and evidence.

It is easier to see this in practice. Consider what is wrong with the following argument:

> **Comprehensive schools are widely supported because they are designed to give all students equal access to learning. Yet most of them are streamed. In order to ensure that all pupils have the same education, it is inappropriate to set them into different ability groups, so all comprehensives should reject the idea of streaming their students.**

You should be able to see that the concepts of 'equal access to learning' and 'same education' are conflated. People agreeing that all local children of the appropriate age should be allowed equal access to the same local school would not necessarily expect them all to have exactly the same education (lessons) when they got there, regardless of their abilities and interests. The conclusion can be reached only if we accept that all pupils should have the 'same education' and this has not been established by the reasoning in the first sentence, even though careless reading might suggest that it has.

## Problems with cause and effect

Many arguments rest on the assumption that, if two factors are found to **correlate**, one has caused the other.

For example, legislation about homosexual acts has been gradually liberalised since 1967 and at the same time the rate of teenage pregnancy has increased, yet it would be totally illogical, for obvious reasons, to argue that the increased pregnancies are due to greater homosexual activity.

> **Correlation** means different factors going up or down at the same rate over time — positive correlation — or one factor going up as the other goes down — negative correlation.

Nevertheless you will find arguers using correlations as evidence that juvenile crime has increased since more women have undertaken paid work and concluding that we should discourage women from working, to reduce the juvenile crime rate. This is not to say that there can never be **causal links** between factors that correlate. Divorce has increased over the same period that fewer people have attended places of worship and it *may* be that divorcees are less concerned about the ethics of dissolving their marriages than people in the past who made what they felt were binding vows before God. But we cannot be sure of this link simply because there is a correlation. We would need to seek further evidence to establish cause and effect. This flaw in reasoning is sometimes known as **correlation equals cause confusion**.

Alternatively the more general term **false cause** could be used. This describes any situation in which a factor or event is claimed to have caused another, without appropriate evidence being supplied, whether or not correlations are involved.

A similar error is to assume the **direction** of cause and effect. If a high proportion of clinically depressed people are found to be unemployed, employers might be accused of discriminating against those with mental illnesses. However, it might be that the people's depression resulted from their unemployment and not the other way round. This is best described as **confusing cause and effect**.

Another error is the **oversimplifying of causal relationships**. It was suggested above that the UK increase in divorce could potentially be linked with lower rates of attendance at places of worship. However, to claim a simple case of cause and effect would be quite wrong. For one thing, attendance at places of worship is not a clear indicator of attitudes. People may attend because they are expected to or may not attend despite having faith. Also, there are multiple causes for the increase in divorce, including changes in legislation that have made it easier, legal aid and greater opportunities for women to work and therefore cope independently. To ascribe any effect to one simple cause is often poor reasoning.

## Reasoning from wrong actions

Revised

This common type of flaw involves an attempt to justify a wrong action because others are committing one. Strictly speaking, there are two variations.

- The Latin phrase *tu quoque* means 'you too'. The flaw involves deflecting what might be sound criticism by accusing the critic or other people of being guilty of the same fault. For example, if the police stopped you for driving over the speed limit, you might try arguing that the police also exceed the limit.
- 'Two wrongs don't make a right' refers to the arguer maintaining that he or she is justified in committing one wrong act, such as sitting in a first class train seat with a second class ticket, because others commit similar offences, such as not paying the fare at all.

## Confusing necessary and sufficient conditions

Revised

A necessary condition is one that is vital in order for something to happen, e.g. a university might say in its prospectus that an A-level in physics is necessary to be considered for an engineering degree course. A sufficient condition is one that guarantees that the next step can follow. For example, that same university might make you an offer that, providing you get an A in physics and mathematics and at least a B in chemistry and critical thinking, it will accept you. You should be able to see the difference between the minimum without which you have no hope of being considered (necessary) and the considerably greater achievement that is enough (sufficient) to guarantee you a place. The common mistake here is for optimists to think that, because they have the minimum necessary qualification, this will be sufficient to admit them.

Some restaurants have a sign up to say that, to be admitted, men must wear ties. It is unlikely though that they would be welcomed wearing only ties!

## Generalisation

Revised ☐

This is a broad claim based on evidence or experience that is too limited. A sensational headline from a national newspaper in April 2008 is an example:

> **Cheap drugs, satellite TV, free telephone calls and breakfast in bed, no wonder...**
>
> **CRIMINALS BREAK IN TO OUR SOFT JAILS**

This story was based on one drug dealer climbing over the wall of Everthorpe Prison in Yorkshire in order to pass drugs to inmates. By using the word 'jails' in the plural, the newspaper is suggesting the situation is far more widespread that it really is. (It is also implying false cause, giving the impression that criminals break in to prison because it is luxurious enough for them to want to stay there, whereas in fact the dealer in question climbed in only to do business.) This example is known as a **hasty generalisation**, because it reaches a conclusion too quickly, on the basis of one example.

Another version is the **sweeping generalisation** such as:

> **Frenchmen eat garlic and wear striped jumpers.**

In this case a universal statement (implying all Frenchmen) is being made based on a stereotype or a limited number of cases.

In the examination you are most likely to encounter generalisations when an argument is based on evidence from a small survey sample or a single example.

> **Exam tip**
>
> Ensure that you can differentiate between hasty generalisation and sweeping generalisation.

## Straw person (also known as 'straw man')

Revised ☐

Straw person (also known as 'straw man') refers to exaggerating a possible drawback of a proposed scheme or some less attractive attribute of some of its supporters and using this as a reason for dismissing the whole scheme without further examination. The name is metaphorical. It relates to the notion of building up a large, very fragile model of just one negative aspect of the argument (like a man of straw) and then blowing it down. This is poor reasoning because very good schemes may have one or two weaknesses, for instance there may be minority groups for whom exemptions have to be made, but the ideas should be considered on the strength of their merits as well as their limitations. Here is an example:

> Imagine how many people would die in accidents and fires and of critical medical conditions if the emergency services were allowed to respond to their calls for help by driving only at less than 20 miles per hour. We would be little better than murderers if we imposed these restrictions on those rushing to help others. We should strongly oppose any attempt to impose speed limits on motorists.

In this example, the arguer has not considered any of the advantages of speed restrictions on roads, only a disadvantage that applies in a special case. This is not a sound reason for abandoning speed restrictions, as it is possible to make an exception in the case of emergency vehicles.

## Ad hominem
Revised

Meaning 'to the man' in Latin, *ad hominem* refers to criticising some irrelevant feature of the arguer so that listeners dismiss his or her argument without giving it serious consideration. Such comments are frequently made in the House of Commons. When an MP makes a suggestion for new legislation, opponents sometimes remind listeners of one of his or her previous misjudgements rather than considering the new idea on its merits. While this might be a reasonable response if the proposed legislation resembles a scheme mishandled by that MP in the past, it is not valid for a completely different proposal. It might be that the attack is about a sexual scandal, whereas the MP's suggestion is about road building.

**Typical mistakes**

Students sometimes confuse *ad hominem* and straw person because both ignore an argument's merits. However *ad hominem* suggests something unworthy about the idea's proposer whereas straw man exaggerates one of its limitations. Sometimes there is overlap when fun is poked at the more eccentric members of an organisation, implying thereby that its beliefs must be as odd as its members.

# Appeals

An appeal is a reference made in an attempt to persuade people to accept an argument. For example, you might appeal to your listeners' humanity to support your fund-raising efforts to help earthquake victims. In critical thinking, appeals are sometimes divided between misdirected appeals and emotional appeals, though there can be a degree of overlap.

## Misdirected or irrelevant appeals
Revised

Misdirected or irrelevant appeals may mislead us by using evidence inappropriately to support an argument. They include the following.

### Appeal to authority
Appeal to authority is an attempt to support a conclusion on the basis that a well-known figure believes it. The claim may be weakened if the celebrity is not an expert in that particular field or if there could be other experts holding an opposing view. Sometimes the authority said to support the claim is not named, so it is impossible to check the credentials of the 'expert'.

## Appeal to tradition

Appeal to tradition is usually used to oppose a suggested change. The arguer suggests that something that has served us well in the past should not be phased out. However, it may be that the old way of doing things is not appropriate to current circumstances. This appeal is often tinged with emotion, nostalgia for the past. However, also beware of its opposite — the **appeal to novelty**, much loved by advertisers. New products are not automatically better than old ones.

## Appeal to history

Although appeal to history is sometimes used instead of 'appeal to tradition', it has a second usage. This is where evidence about what happened in the past is used to predict future performance or behaviour. This may influence decisions that are made, for example, to avert an impending crisis. While it might seem sensible to 'learn from our past mistakes', exactly the same situation rarely if ever recurs. Tactics used to counter an international threat in one century might not necessarily be effective in the next. Britain reduced the problem of prison overcrowding in previous centuries by transporting convicts to Australia but it is not a practical solution in the twenty-first century.

## Appeal to popularity

Sometimes known as the appeal to common practice, appeal to popularity uses weight of numbers as evidence that a claim must be true or a type of behaviour acceptable. History is full of examples of wide-scale human error, such as the belief that the earth was flat, and of massive moral aberration, such as the Nazi holocaust and the slave trade. Clearly the fact that many people believe or endorse something does not guarantee that it is true or right.

## Emotional appeals

Revised

While the appeals above are often misdirected, they can be logical and legitimate in some circumstances, such as appealing to an authority with really relevant expertise or electing the most popular candidate after a ballot. In contrast, emotional appeals make no attempt to use logic. To escape criticism arguments must always be supported by sound reasoning and evidence.

Political leaflets and broadcasts sometimes appeal to our sense of **fear**, using scare tactics about the folly of the ruling party to persuade us to support a rival. Political speakers sometimes use an incident such as a high-profile murder as a 'political football' to kick around in public, creating a moral panic out of proportion to the problem. Sometimes this is accompanied by an appeal to **prejudice** or **stereotypes** and an appeal to **hatred** or **indignation**.

An appeal to **pity**, unaccompanied by sound reasons why you should support the claimant's point of view, is usually unworthy of consideration. Alternatively people might try to persuade you to their side by flattering you, perhaps by suggesting that they know you are perceptive enough to see the truth, an appeal to **vanity**. Language that attempts to manipulate emotion is known as **loaded** and the term **rant** refers to a persuasive passage that expresses strong emotion without coherent reasoning.

On the other hand well-reasoned arguments, such as those in some pressure group or charity leaflets, might arouse a certain amount of feeling as well as providing compelling evidence why we should support their cause.

**Now test yourself**
Tested

2  Identify the appeals in the following extract:

**The UK legal system allows ANY mother to stop contact between a child and its father, without any punishment whatsoever. Thousands of children and dads suffer because some mothers think that it is ok to abuse their children by denying them access to their own parent.**

(Adapted from a website on rights for fathers)

# Other types of evaluation

**Assessing the use of evidence**
Revised

In Unit 2 you may be asked to explain weaknesses in the use of evidence in a paragraph. Look back at the Unit 1 section on evaluating statistics and research evidence (pp. 13–14) to remind yourself of some ways in which they can be misleading. The passage below offers some other reasons why the statistics for girl crime cannot be taken at face value.

**Now test yourself**
Tested

3  Read the passage below and list as many reasons as you can why the proportion of girls committing crime might appear misleadingly high in statistics.

**Why girls are committing more crimes**

**A report today showing a sharp increase in crimes committed by girls has prompted researchers to investigate the underlying causes of this trend. Preliminary research, conducted by London's South Bank University, suggested a number of contributing factors. One reason might simply be that the overall population of girls has increased and therefore the number of crimes committed by this population could be expected to rise proportionally.**

**According to Susannah Eagle at South Bank, the statistics released by the Youth Justice Board only took into consideration the absolute number of crimes committed by girls and not offences per person. 'It is very possible, therefore, that there might not be more girls committing offences, but that some girls are prolific offenders,' she said. The rise in reported crimes could also be due to changing social attitudes. Eagle suggested there was now a lower tolerance of minor offences.**

**Underage drinking could also be a factor. When the research team interviewed a sample group of girls who had committed a crime, there was a statistically significant link between committing a violent offence and the recent use of alcohol.**

**According to Enver Solomon, deputy director of the Centre for Crime and Justice Studies, 'Police are under pressure to hit certain targets. Offences committed by kids — such as fights between girls in the playground — would be more likely to be recorded now than a few years ago.'**

(Extract from 'Why girls are committing more crimes' by Elizabeth Stewart, *Guardian*, 15 May 2008, www.guardian.co.uk, reproduced by permission of Guardian News & Media Ltd)

## Assessing analogies

Using analogies in arguments involves creation of parallels, reasoning that what is true for one situation must be true of another that is, supposedly, similar. Evaluating an analogy requires you to gauge whether the situations being compared really are similar enough for the conclusion to be reached. Read the following passage, which contains an analogy, and try to form an initial judgement.

> Britain has very strict laws about testing the health of domestic pets before letting them into the country. Even British people living in France, whenever they want to take their dog to Britain for a few days, have to take it to the vet's in order to have its health checked and a certificate issued. The code on the certificate has to correspond with a microchip in the dog to avoid the possibility of fraud. With the increased incidence in Britain of diseases such as tuberculosis, prevalent abroad but virtually eradicated here until recently, there is an obvious need for compulsory health checks and certification for people entering the country, even if they are British and have been away for a few days on holiday.

Questions about analogies often come in pairs. Consider the following questions:

1 Identify what is being compared in the analogy in the paragraph above. (2 marks)

2 How well does the analogy support the author's argument? (3 marks)

To answer question 2:

● Discuss important ways in which the situations are similar and dissimilar, identifying at least one point for each.

● If you decide the situations being compared are less similar than the writer implies, state that the differences are significant enough to outweigh the similarities.

● Occasionally the initial statement about the supposedly uncontroversial situation is inaccurate, meaning the analogy is unconvincing from the start.

● Conclude by stating whether the writer provided a persuasive and effective analogy, where the parallels are convincing, or a **disanalogy** (a poor analogy) that fails to support the argument.

An answer to question 2 might argue that:

● Domestic pets and people are similar in that both can have communicable diseases that present a health risk to others.

● However, there are significant differences in the situation.

● A relatively small number of pets travel to and fro and, because this is a fairly unusual situation, their owners are prepared to put up with the expense and trouble incurred. In contrast a high proportion of the British public go abroad on holidays and for work and there would be major protests if health checks were introduced. The inconvenience would outweigh the risks.

● We have different attitudes to animal rights and to human rights and dignity. Animals are unable to object to having microchips inserted whereas many humans would.

● These differences outweigh the similarities between the two situations, making the analogy a weak one that therefore fails to support the argument.

### Now test yourself

4 Which of the answers below is the more precise answer to question 1?

a Animals are being compared to people.

b The need for precautions preventing animals bringing diseases into Britain is likened to the need for similar precautions for people entering Britain.

A **disanalogy** is a failed analogy.

A convincing answer reaching the opposite conclusion as a result of finding more parallels between the situations would be equally rewarded.

## Evaluating examples

Revised

Evaluating examples requires similar skills to evaluating analogies. Consider whether the example is:

- typical and relevant enough to support the reasoning well
- an unusual one, with the result that readers need further examples before accepting the conclusion
- so ill-chosen that it acts as a **counter-example**, undermining the reasoning.

Consider this example:

> **British and US politicians aren't evil people, they just think their country would be a terrible mess without them. They begin to think they're so valuable they become prepared to do bad things to stay in power. You can see that with Robert Mugabe. If he'd quit 15 years ago, he'd still be the hero of liberation of Zimbabwe. Instead he's a monster.**
>
> (Gavin Esler in *Metro*, 15 May 2008, reproduced by permission of Solo Syndication)

> **A counter-example** undermines reasoning instead of supporting it.

This is really an analogy rather than an example, as Mugabe is not a British or US politician but an African leader. The example is poor in other ways, because Mugabe's behaviour is so extreme that it cannot reasonably be likened to any actions British and US politicians are known to have made to retain their positions. The reader is likely to require further examples closer to home to be convinced that our politicians 'become prepared to do bad things to stay in power'. This example therefore, because it is so untypical, serves little purpose, except as an emotional appeal.

## Evaluating explanations and suggesting alternatives

Revised

Unit 2 sometimes requires you to assess explanations, in the form of multiple-choice options or in a longer passage, or to offer reasonable alternatives. Consider the four explanations for the trends in divorce given below.

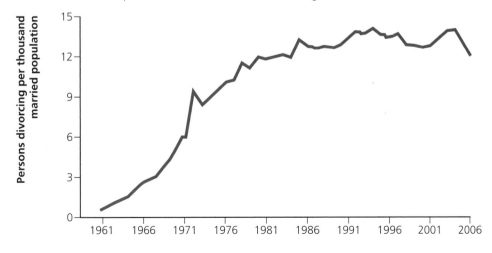

*Divorces in England and Wales, including annulments*
Source: **www.statistics.gov.uk**

Which of the following statements is the *least* convincing explanation of the trends shown in the graph, which shows the number of divorces granted each year per thousand married population?

a   The number of divorces may have increased during the 1960s in response to growing feminist awareness, which could have encouraged married women to question their situations.

b   The Divorce Reform Act passed in 1969 in England and Wales came into effect in 1971. As this made divorce easier, it explains the steep peak in divorces in 1971.

c   The brief downturn in the number of divorces around 1973 could be explained because most of those who had been waiting for divorces for some years had acted quickly when the Divorce Reform Act was implemented.

d   The steady decline in church-going during the twentieth century is reflected in increased divorce, as people are less concerned than they used to be about keeping vows made before God.

The correct answer is (d). Although there has been a steady decline in church attendance, the graph does not indicate a steady increase in divorce but a much more varied pattern. The other answers offer better explanations for specific patterns in the graph. In addition, decline in church-going does not necessarily indicate a loss of religious beliefs and in Britain a proportion of the population attends other places of worship.

> **Now test yourself**
>
> 5   Suggest two possible explanations that could be offered for a steady decline in the divorce rate since the early 1990s (this time ignoring any irregularities in the graph).
>
> Tested ☐

> **Typical mistakes**
>
> Students often confuse numbers with rates. Rates refer to proportions, such as the number per thousand of the population. Population changes are likely to affect the number of people acting in a certain way but not necessarily the rate.

## Assessing hypothetical reasoning

Revised ☐

Unit 1 explained that predictions about the outcome of possible future conditions are based on guesswork so can provide only limited support to reasoning. For example:

> If the rate of obesity increases at its present rate, then we shall soon need to redesign furniture and seating in public transport to accommodate bigger people.

In fact this may not be necessary, as obesity rates may fall as people learn more about its risks and how to avoid it.

Hypothesising about how the present might have turned out if the past had been different is even more fruitless, as this is speculation about something that has no basis in reality.

A different type of hypothetical reasoning that is sometimes known as **suppositional reasoning** may be more worthwhile. It is used by scientists, doctors and detectives and other types of investigators.

> Suppose that the murderer had entered and left the scene of the crime via the window. If that were the case then the window would not be locked from the inside, unless the murderer had an accomplice, which has been ruled out. However, investigation has revealed that the window was locked from the inside. The murderer must then have taken a different route or still be in the building.

This type of hypothesis is based on deduction about alternative real-life possibilities.

When assessing the extent to which hypothetical reasoning supports an argument, you will need to judge whether it is based on ill-informed guesswork or a more logical process of considering the evidence for a series of different possibilities.

Now test yourself

Tested

6 Assess the usefulness of the hypothetical reasoning in the following examples:

a Doctor: 'If my patient had disease A then he would be likely to exhibit symptoms X and Y. As he has no such symptoms, then I should ask about other symptoms that match a different diagnosis.'

b If the superpowers had not armed themselves with nuclear deterrents after the Second World War then we should not have enjoyed over half a century without a world war.

## Assessing the relevance of general principles

Revised

As well as asking you to identify principles, instructions may tell you to:

● evaluate the extent to which a principle supports an argument
● assess the extent to which a principle applies to another situation
● explain where a general principle would not be applicable

If there were a passage about people protesting in public, you should be able to identify that the right to do this in Britain reflects the principle of free speech. What other situations can you think of where such a principle applies?

Good examples would be UK radio and television interviews, where people likely to express contrasting views are invited to put them forward. The freedom of the press and the rights of victims to express their feelings at the end of a court case are further examples.

## Now test yourself

Tested

7 Think of a situation in Britain where the principle that we should be entitled to free speech would not be upheld.

In this question you need to do some creative thinking, seeking examples from your own general knowledge, unless relevant situations are mentioned in the passage.

Answers on p. 103–104

## Check your understanding

Tested

1 What is the difference between a post hoc flaw and correlation equals cause confusion?

2 What is the difference between the flaws of *tu quoque* and 'two wrongs don't make a right'?

3 Explain what is meant by confusing necessary and sufficient conditions.

4 How do hasty and sweeping generalisations differ?

5 In February 2011 Colonel Gaddafi of Libya refused to consider the demands of protesters against his regime, saying they were drug-takers. Name the common flaw in his comment.

6 What is another name for false dichotomy?

7 Why is an appeal to history often misdirected?

8 Identify the weakness in the following argument: 'For centuries we have hunted foxes. There is no reason why we should give it up now.'

9 Name the appeal that suggests that we should accept the opinion of the majority.

10 What is a disanalogy?

11 What is meant by a conclusion being overdrawn?

12 What is a counter-example?

Answers on p. 104

## Exam practice

Read the following passage and then answer the questions that follow. (Please note: (a) to (c) are analysis questions; (d) is an evaluation question.)

**Learning from Japan**

**In Britain a couple of centuries ago, happy families sat together telling stories in the firelight. Now we are entirely dependent on electricity and families are fragmented, adults watching television downstairs while children play on bedroom computers. Divorce has escalated as a result.**

**The damage to Japanese nuclear power stations as a result of the 2011 earthquake should teach us a lesson. An earthquake in Britain could similarly wreck our nuclear installations, leading to toxic leaks, a massive death toll and the contamination of farming land for centuries. Though some argue that Britain is not as prone to earthquakes as Japan, they are still a frequent occurrence. In February 2008 an earthquake with Lincolnshire as its epicentre was strong enough to be felt as far away as Ireland. Though no one was killed, a 19-year-old in Yorkshire was injured as a chimney fell through the roof onto his bed.**

**Clearly nuclear power carries significant risks and we should prioritise safety over materialism. If we are not prepared to face losing a significant proportion of our population in a nuclear accident, we must learn to live without electricity, as our forefathers did.**

**a** Identify the counter-assertion in the argument. [3]

**b** Identify the general principle in the argument. [3]

**c** 'Clearly nuclear power carries significant risks'. Identify what component of argument this is and explain your answer. [3]

**d** Evaluate the reasoning in the passage. (You should refer to three strengths and/or weaknesses, using technical terms, making specific quotations or references to the passage and explaining why each is a strength or weakness. Reach a conclusion about whether the argument is predominantly strong or weak.) [9]

## Answers online

Online

## Exam summary

- There may be up to about 9 marks available for evaluating the reasoning in a passage, with about 3 marks for each developed point. The amount of space allocated indicates the amount of detail required.
- Strike a balance between completing the paper in time and answering so briefly that you score only half marks for questions to which you know the answer.
- Try answering in writing a variety of questions from Unit 2 papers and then comparing your work with examples on mark schemes (on OCR website). This will indicate whether your answers are too brief or unnecessarily long and time-wasting. This is essential knowledge, as completing the paper is as important as thoroughness.
- Bullet point suggestions may be provided for guidance.
- Brush up your skills in identifying the best statement of the flaw in a passage from options such as *ad hominem* and straw person.
- You will need to recall the elements of argument covered in Unit 1, such as conclusion, reason, indicator, evidence, example, counter-argument and assumption. In addition you should be able to identify and explain

the purpose of the following components within an argument in the source material:
- intermediate conclusion
- analogy
- general principle
- The specification requires you to be able to explain the difference between an explanation, an argument and pieces of writing that lack the structure of either. You should also be able to demonstrate understanding of the following terms and use them accurately according to their usage in critical thinking:
- counter
- challenge
- assess
- opinion
- belief
- knowledge
- reasoning
- refute
- repudiate

- infer and inference
- contradict and contradiction
- coherent
- structure
- strength and weakness
- support
- inconsistent and inconsistency
- consistent
- imply
- converse
- ambiguous
- drawing a conclusion

✔ The best answers include specialist vocabulary, so use the correct terms for flaws and strengths.

✔ Usually it is necessary to quote the example of the flaw, explain how it can be recognised in this context and why it is poor reasoning. You should be able to identify flaws in the resource material by name and clarify how you have recognised them in this particular context.

✔ Sometimes, as in the case of unjustified assumptions, it is useful to indicate what the truth might be.

✔ You will be expected to evaluate parts of the argument in the document, identifying strengths and weaknesses in its reasoning. In doing so, you should demonstrate an understanding of the difference between challenging reasoning with counter-arguments or alternative explanations, and the more complex skill of explaining the strengths and weaknesses of the original reasoning.

✔ You may need to evaluate arguments by drawing on types of evaluation introduced in Unit 1, such as assessing the use of evidence.

## Appeals

✔ You should be able to identify an 'appeal', a rhetorical device swaying the audience by emotional persuasion rather than by rational argument. This means it may not support the conclusion of an argument as effectively as logical reasoning. Ensure that you can identify by name and describe the appeals within arguments.

## Evaluation

You should be able to assess strengths and weaknesses in arguments by:

✔ assessing the use of evidence in the form of survey and other research data, statistics (percentages or proportions), statistical representations (average or mean) and other numerical information (this is also required for Unit 1)

✔ evaluating the use of analogies within arguments by:

- identifying the situations compared in the analogy and the conclusion drawn from the parallel reasoning
- identifying similarities and dissimilarities between the situations and assessing their significance
- reaching a judgement about whether the analogy is strong enough to support the conclusion drawn in the argument

✔ identifying and assessing examples used in the argument, by commenting on the relevance of the example (which may be good or poor, even a counter-example), and by assessing the degree to which the example helps the author to make the point

✔ identifying explanations given within an argument and offering reasonable alternatives

✔ suggesting other conclusions that could reasonably be drawn from evidence used in an argument

✔ assessing the extent to which any hypothetical reasoning supports an argument

✔ assessing the extent to which general principles apply in other situations and explaining where a general principle would not be applicable

✔ identifying any assumptions that, if unjustified, weaken the conclusion

# 5 Developing your own arguments

Section C of the Unit 2 paper requires some creative thinking, going beyond information that is provided in the passage, as well as good skills in written communication (AO3). To start with you may be required to perform one or two short writing tasks, making suggestions that in some way relate to the documents you have just read or a similar but new situation.

Likely tasks include writing:

- a possible explanation for a phenomenon mentioned in the documents
- an additional reason beyond those given in the documents
- several reasons to support a given claim not in the documents
- a detailed example of a problem that might arise in a given scenario

To succeed in this task:

- Ensure that your answer is clear and full enough to merit the 2 or 3 marks available.
- Write in full sentences, using the appropriate components required — for example, an explanation has a reason and a conclusion.
- Make sure that your answer is plausible (reasonable and likely).

## Writing your own arguments

Your main tasks will be to write your own arguments, usually two.

These arguments usually carry 12 marks each, so keep a close eye on the time throughout the examination. If you are falling behind, write the arguments well before the end and then return to the remaining lower-mark questions.

### Tackling the questions
Revised

One question may ask you to construct a further argument either challenging or supporting the main conclusion of the passage. As you will not be told what the conclusion is, it is important not to confuse it with the intermediate conclusion, although a good argument based on the wrong conclusion should still gain some marks.

Alternatively a conclusion may be provided on a different though usually related subject. In either case, use this exact wording in your argument. Students often drift to a conclusion that is similar to but not exactly the same as the one provided, for example from discouraging cars to banning them; such inaccuracy is penalised.

Others forget to include the conclusion as they have mentioned it in their title, losing marks as a result.

Writing a **further** argument means that you must not repeat the reasons, evidence or examples used in the documents. The only situation in which this is acceptable is to take an ambiguous piece of evidence and cleverly reinterpret it in a different way from the original argument.

If given a choice, it may be easier to challenge the argument in the passage than to support it, as many of the most obvious reasons supporting it will already have been given.

Make your decision totally clear to the examiner by heading your work 'An argument challenging…' or 'An argument supporting…', rather than adopting a more imaginative title.

You will be told which components or elements your argument should include. These are likely to be:

- a main conclusion
- three or more reasons that support an intermediate or main conclusion
- an intermediate conclusion
- use of evidence or examples to support the argument
- counter-assertion or counter-argument

and possibly elements such as:

- hypothetical reasoning
- a general principle
- an analogy

Ensure that you include all the components listed in the instructions. If you have time, it is advisable to supply more than the bare minimum. Your work will be allocated to a mark band and the highest level requires the candidate to supply a developed argument that contains 'at least' three reasons, 'at least' one intermediate conclusion and so on. A fuller argument is therefore welcomed, providing it is carefully constructed and convincing.

Do not spend so long on the first argument that you are unable to complete the second. Assume you have at most 15 minutes to write each argument.

Plan a clear structure for your argument before you start writing. A long, confused ramble will not be well rewarded. Make jottings in pencil on the blank part of the answer sheet, crossing it through neatly afterwards.

You are not expected to have extensive prior knowledge of the topic set. In choosing evidence or examples, draw on your own general knowledge.

The convincing nature of your arguments will be judged as well as the structure, so avoid including flippant reasons and evidence that is clearly made up.

A top-band argument must rely only on one or two reasonable assumptions. The reasons, evidence and examples must fully support the intermediate conclusions and overall conclusion.

**Typical mistakes**

A typical mistake is to write an argument supporting a slightly different conclusion from the one stipulated. Another is to use reasoning or evidence already employed in the documents.

**Typical mistakes**

A typical mistake is to employ reasoning that provides only limited support for the conclusion.

Adopt an academic tone. Avoid using flowery language, rhetorical questions, humour, appeals to emotion and other dramatic features of style that might be rewarded in an English essay.

Using concise and convincing analogies or well-chosen principles as part of the reasoning is likely to be rewarded.

Check your work for accuracy of grammar, spelling and punctuation as these are assessed in this part of the paper.

Unless a different structure is specified, examiners are likely to be impressed by a sound argument with the following or similar components, clearly structured as follows:

● CA (a counter-conclusion supported by a counter-reason)
● R1 (challenging the counter-argument)
● R2 (supporting main argument)
● Ex
● IC1
● R3 (supporting main argument)
● Ev
● IC2
● C

One or two more reasons with further evidence and examples would probably be rewarded if you had time, but this depends on how long you spend on the rest of the paper and how natural you find composing arguments.

> **Exam tip**
>
> It is better to complete two short arguments that fulfil the minimum requirements than to be unable to complete the examination. A compromise if you do not have many minutes left could be to construct your first argument based on the minimum requirements and to make the second argument more complex if time permits.

## Planning your arguments

Revised

A useful tip for planning your argument is to work backwards from the conclusion you want to support. For example, suppose this is:

**Education should be made compulsory to the age of 18.**

Let us suppose that you have sufficient time left to write a sophisticated argument worthy of top level marks. As two intermediate conclusions will show your ability to create a sophisticated argument, think of two major, broad reasons that could support the conclusion. These could be:

**Education for self-development**

and

**Benefits to the economy**

If these are going to be your **intermediate conclusions**, you need to think of reasons that could support these. Try breaking down the notion of education for self-development into two elements. These could be gaining independent study skills and preparation for everyday life. These ideas could be phrased as **reasons**, but they will need **examples** or **evidence** to support them.

Once you have worked that out, consider how you could work back from the other intermediate conclusion about benefits to the economy. Think of two relevant factors that can be developed into reasons, with some examples or evidence you have perhaps heard in the media.

Before we put it all together, a **counter-argument** is needed, followed by a reason to challenge it. How about referring to the fact that many young people dislike school?

> **Exam tip**
>
> Although OCR instructions often do not specify a counter-assertion or counter-argument, it is advisable to include one.

## Now test yourself                                            Tested ▢

1 Using the hints above, write an argument supporting the conclusion that 'Education should be made compulsory to the age of 18.' Set out each component on a new line and annotate it (with CA, R1 etc.) to help structure it clearly.

   Time yourself to see whether it takes you 15 minutes or longer. If it takes longer, include fewer components in your next argument while still covering the minimum required by the question.

Answers on p. 104

## Timing sections of the paper

It is essential to practise answering examination papers several times with a strict time limit, checking how long you spend on each section so you are not caught out. Unless instructions change, *and you must check this*, the recommended time for completing sections B and C of the Unit 2 paper is 1 hour and 10 minutes. Sections B and C carry similar marks, so it is worth putting a considerable amount of effort into your arguments in section C. Try a section B question and see if you can complete it in 30–35 minutes. Assuming it takes you 5 minutes to complete one or two low-mark questions in section C, this should then leave you about 30 minutes to divide between the two arguments.

## Check your understanding                                      Tested ▢

1 Suggest three weaknesses that you should guard against when writing arguments of your own.

Answers on p. 104

## Exam practice

Try writing an argument in timed conditions, using a similar structure to the one above in Now test yourself 1.      [12]

As well as having a title stating explicitly which option you have chosen, your argument must include:

● a main conclusion worded exactly as in the question

● at least three reasons that support an intermediate or main conclusion

● at least one intermediate conclusion

● use of evidence or examples to support the reasons

Identify each element of your argument with the usual notations and ask a teacher or an able fellow student to check it and give you feedback. Your argument could support or challenge one of the following conclusions, the last of which is a general principle:

● The age for buying and consuming alcohol should be raised to 21.

● The government was right to increase the age for purchasing cigarettes to 18.

● The voting age should be reduced to 16.

- People should be encouraged to become vegetarians.
- Secondary schools should have compulsory lessons on good parenting.
- Prisoners should not be allowed to vote.
- All schools should be single sex.
- Understanding offenders' motivation is more crucial than increasing penalties.

Keep working at this to see how elaborate a structure you can manage in the time allocation of about 15 minutes.

Because of the variety of tasks here, model answers are not supplied, but you can check your work against these OCR criteria for a top-level argument:

- Candidates present their own relevant further argument with a clear structure that includes at least three reasons and at least one properly supported intermediate conclusion.
- The argument is persuasive and relies on only one or two reasonable assumptions.
- The argument will also contain evidence/examples that support the argument.
- There may be a counter-argument/counter-examples.
- The final conclusion is precisely stated.
- Grammar, spelling and punctuation are good. Errors are few.

**Answers and Unit 2 quick quiz online**

Online

## Exam summary

✔ In section C there may be a couple of lower-mark questions inviting you to draw on your own ideas to provide explanations, further examples or reasons for something mentioned in the passage.

✔ However, your main task will be to write your own arguments (AO3), usually two, that relate to the conclusion of the argument in the document or an allied theme. You may have to challenge or support the conclusion of the stimulus passage or a conclusion stated in the question. Clear structure is important as well as ensuring that the content of an argument clearly supports the conclusion given with only a few reasonable assumptions being needed.

✔ To score high marks your argument needs to include a range of argument components, for example:
- three or more reasons that support an intermediate or main conclusion
- at least one intermediate conclusion
- the conclusion
- evidence or examples to support the reasons

- counter-assertion or counter-argument
- possibly elements such as sound hypothetical reasoning, general principle or convincing analogy

✔ It is important to:
- plan to ensure that your argument is logically organised and made up of recognisable components
- support the precise conclusion required, not a variation
- state in your title what the purpose of your argument is (supporting or challenging what conclusion)
- use convincing reasons and evidence drawn from your own general knowledge, not ones from the passage
- write in an academic tone, avoiding appeals to emotion, rhetorical questions and other literary devices, attempts at humour and 'flowery' language

# 6 Identifying problems in ethical reasoning

# Answering the short questions

Documents accompanying the Unit 3 examination present facts and views about a controversial issue relating to medical ethics, crime and punishment, the environment, or another area of social or political concern. The examination begins with several questions requiring short answers, followed by an essay applying a range of criteria to potential decisions and a longer essay reaching a judgement about which course of action to take by applying ethical principles. As the bulk of the marks are awarded for these two essays, it is important not to spend more than a few minutes on the short questions.

## Analysing problems of definition
Revised ☐

One of the first Unit 3 questions may ask you to suggest and explain problems of defining a particular term crucial to the issue being discussed. Different documents may include explicit but contradictory definitions, or the key term may be used without definition, leaving you to infer the intended shade of meaning, which again is likely to vary between documents.

To answer this:

- Suggest two or more different meanings.
- Identify two or more reasons *why* the usages differ.

Usages may vary for the following reasons:

- People holding varying moral or political views may interpret abstract concepts such as 'rights', 'freedom' and 'duty' differently.
- Different subject specialisms and professions use some terms differently from each other and from the general public, e.g. students of critical thinking use the word 'assumption' differently from other people. A mouse is a different thing to a computer user and a pet owner.
- Problems arise in applying terminology across cultures. A lifestyle that is regarded as 'poor' in the UK might seem like relative wealth in sub-Saharan Africa. This is described as cultural relativism.
- Contexts influence word usage. Is driving 1 mph over the limit speeding? What about driving just below the legal limit but in hazardous conditions such as fog, when the norm is to go far more slowly?
- In some instances, such as with 'unemployment' and 'poverty', official definitions used by particular governments change over time.
- Words may be used in slightly different ways by people vague about their precise meanings.

> **Exam tip**
>
> Your study of ambiguity at AS should help with this task.

> **Typical mistakes**
>
> Candidates often supply only one point when a question asks for 'problems' or 'reasons'. The mark scheme is likely to divide the marks across two or more suggestions so a single point, however detailed, is unlikely to earn full marks.

Usually you should be able to infer these different possibilities from the sources, though sometimes a little creative thinking is needed.

Consider the moral concept of fairness. Under recent legislation anyone over the age of 16 caught carrying a knife will face automatic prosecution and risk a jail sentence of up to 4 years. Supposing a person whose job it is to lay linoleum and carpets was searched by the police on his way to work and charged with possessing a knife. One media report might describe this as fair as the law must apply equally to all. However, another could object that knives are the usual tool for cutting lino and it is unfair to prosecute workers for carrying the necessities of a legal trade. In this context you would need to refer to the two documents and explain that 'fair' can mean equal treatment for all or it can refer to reasonable operation of the law, if necessary allowing for cases of special need. The problem here arises from the ambiguity of the word 'fair'.

**Now test yourself**

1 Why might civil rights supporters and prison officers have different uses of the term 'freedom'?

Answers on p. 104

Tested

## Questions of measurement

Revised

A fairly frequent low-mark question is one that asks about difficulties of measuring a particular phenomenon. This entails deciding how you would recognise the phenomenon in the first place, as well as considering how you would measure its extent.

To practise this skill, read the two documents below and then consider this question, which will be discussed below:

**What problems might arise in using document 1 to measure the extent and scale of obesity?**

Notice that, even though the question refers only to document 1, you may be able to use ideas from document 2 (and other documents on the examination paper) to challenge its suggestions.

**Document 1 Medical terms for obesity**

Obesity traditionally has been defined as a weight at least 20% above the weight corresponding to the lowest death rate for individuals of a specific height, gender, and age (ideal weight). 20–40% over ideal weight is considered mildly obese; 40–100% over ideal weight is considered moderately obese; and 100% over ideal weight is considered severely, or morbidly, obese.

More recent guidelines for obesity use a measurement called BMI (body mass index) which is the individual's weight multiplied by 703 and then divided by twice the height in inches. BMI of 25.9–29 is considered overweight; BMI over 30 is considered obese. Since the BMI describes the body weight relative to height, it correlates strongly (in adults) with the total body fat content. Some very muscular people may have a high BMI without undue health risks.

(Sourced from the Answer.com and MedicineNet.com websites)

**Document 2 The National Association to Advance Fat Acceptance**

Obesity researchers refuse to see that fatness is a cultural issue. When they acknowledge the social stigma involved in fatness, they see the solution as changing body size rather than eradicating the stigma.

Most obesity researchers experience an economic conflict of interest. The 1985 National Institute of Health (NIH) conference which proclaimed obesity a 'killer disease' also arbitrarily redefined obesity in such a way as to affect millions more Americans. This redefinition and the call for treatment translated into vastly increased research funding, weight loss industry profits, and physicians' revenues. The chairman of the conference was a paid consultant to United Weight Control and two doctors considered to be leading authorities in obesity research were paid consultants to the makers of Optifast, a low-calorie diet product.

The National Association to Advance Fat Acceptance (NAAFA) demands that the NIH fund new investigators and studies focussing on non-dieting alternatives to improve the health and well-being of fat people and that fat people have a voice in the types of weight-related issues being researched and the development of public policy about fatness.

(Extract from **www.naafa.org**)

Here is a possible answer:

Document 1 presents statistics-based definitions of obesity. These carry a certain amount of authority because they are couched in scientific language, but the account presents almost too much information because criteria are given for three degrees of obesity, mild to severe. The matter is complicated by an alternative measure, the BMI, more up to date but sometimes misleading for very muscular people. It is therefore unclear whether to use the first set of criteria (assuming we also had figures for ideal weights) or the BMI measurements.

Document 2 casts doubt on both these possibilities, radically suggesting that obesity can be 'arbitrarily redefined' by specialists to enrich the diet industry and medical specialists. This suggests the criteria have no scientific basis and reflect cultural bias. Therefore a fundamental problem of using either of the measures of obesity in document 1 is that these measures may be less objective than they seem, as they could shift according to the whim of professionals with vested interests.

**Exam tip**

Many candidates write too much for low-mark questions, neglecting the higher-mark questions as a consequence. For this type of question examiners reward answers that contain:

- identification of problems of measurement (which might include problems of definition)
- a brief explanation or exploration of the problems
- reference to the documents

This answer would be more than adequate for 6 marks; you would need to be considerably briefer if only 4 marks were available.

## How interpretation differences might affect action

Revised

A likely follow-up question to one about definition or measurement might ask:

**Referring to relevant documents, explain how differences in interpretation of the term 'obesity' might affect the implementation of related social policies.**

The answer seems obvious — if people cannot agree on a definition of the problem, their response will be confused. However, an answer worthy of full marks would entail:

- quoting and explaining clearly differences of interpretation of the term in particular documents
- explaining ways in which each interpretation could affect the pursuit of several specific policies

## Factors that might affect how people react to an issue

Another short question could ask you to identify and explain several factors that might affect how people react to the key issue described in the resources. You should be able to identify different viewpoints in the various documents and work out what it is about these people's background, role, profession, experience or outlook that has influenced their view.

> **Exam tip**
>
> Identify the factors in separate paragraphs. Begin with a concise identification of the factor and then, in the following sentence or two, explain why that factor has influenced the person's or group's attitude according to a specified document.

## Using claims or evidence to oppose or support a proposal

This type of question draws on evaluation skills from the AS course. Questions can take various forms:

- **Suggest and explain briefly one problem of using the evidence in paragraph 1 of document 2 to support proposal X. (3 marks)**
- **Suggest and explain briefly one problem of using claims in document 1 to oppose proposal X. (3 marks)**
- **Suggest and explain briefly two problems in using documents 1 and 2 to inform decision-making about X. You should refer directly to the documents in your answers. (6 marks)**

Even though a particular document may be arguing for a proposal, there are likely to be weaknesses in it, such as:

- reasoning that is inconsistent or hypothetical
- evidence that is outdated, not quite relevant or too selective
- research that may be unrepresentative
- statistics that may be misleading or unreliable
- vested interest or bias by those making claims, such as governments
- unjustified assumptions
- no consideration of counter-arguments
- appeals to emotion or misdirected appeals

> **Exam tip**
>
> Usually, each problem carries 3 marks, 2 of which are earned for clear explanation of the problem and one for relevant reference to the document.

## Check your understanding

1 Suggest why there is a problem of definition concerning the word 'conclusion' when used in critical thinking and in the sentence 'At the conclusion of the concert the audience clapped enthusiastically'.

2 What is meant by cultural relativism? Consider how people from different cultures and backgrounds might differ in how they define 'cruelty to animals' and 'child abuse'.

**Answers on pp. 104–105**

## Exam practice

1 Referring to documents 3, 4 and 5, explain why the term 'war' might present problems of definition. [6]

**Document 3 War**

**War is a violent way for determining who gets to say what goes on in a given territory, for example, regarding: who gets power, who gets wealth and resources, whose ideals prevail, where the border rests and so on. War is the ultimate means for deciding these issues if a peaceful process or resolution can't be agreed upon.**

The mere threat of war, and the presence of mutual disdain between political communities, do not suffice as indicators of war. The conflict of arms must be actual, and not merely latent, for it to count as war. Further, the actual armed conflict must be both intentional and widespread: isolated clashes between rogue officers, or border patrols, do not count as actions of war. The onset of war requires a conscious commitment, and a significant mobilization, on the part of the belligerents in question. There's no real war, so to speak, until the fighters intend to go to war and until they do so with a heavy quantum of force.

(Extracts from the article 'War' from the *Stanford Encyclopedia of Philosophy*, plato.stanford.edu/entries/war, reproduced by permission of Brian Orend and Stanford Encyclopedia)

## Document 4 Cold War and proxy war

The Cold War was the period of conflict, tension and competition between the United States and the Soviet Union and their respective allies from the mid-1940s until the early 1990s. Throughout this period, the rivalry between the two superpowers unfolded in multiple arenas: military coalitions; ideology, psychology, and espionage; sports; military, industrial, and technological developments, including the space race; costly defence spending; a massive conventional and nuclear arms race; and many proxy wars. There was never a direct military engagement between the United States and the Soviet Union, but there was half a century of military build-up as well as political battles for support around the world, including significant involvement of allied and satellite nations in proxy wars.

A proxy war is the war that results when two powers use third parties as substitutes for fighting each other directly. While superpowers have sometimes used whole governments as proxies, terrorist groups, mercenaries, or other third parties are more often employed. It is hoped that these groups can strike an opponent without leading to full-scale war.

(Wikipedia definitions of Cold War and proxy war, en.wikipedia.org)

## Document 5 War on drugs

The War on Drugs is a prohibition campaign undertaken by the United States government with the assistance of participating countries, intended to reduce the illegal drug trade — to curb supply and diminish demand for certain psychoactive substances deemed 'harmful or undesirable' by the government. This initiative includes a set of laws and policies that are intended to discourage the production, distribution and consumption of targeted substances. The term was first used by President Richard Nixon in 1972, and his choice of words was probably based on the War on Poverty, announced by President Lyndon Johnson in 1964.

(Wikipedia definition of War on Drugs, en.wikipedia.org)

**2** Referring to document 1 (p. 52) and documents 6 and 7, explain how differences in interpretation of the term 'obesity' might affect the implementation of related social policies. [6]

## Document 6 Treat child obesity as neglect say doctors

Children under 12 should be taken into care if they are obese, according to doctors.

The call comes after a survey of paediatricians revealed that obesity was a factor in 20 child protection cases last year. Concerns were raised after a BBC investigation found children as young as 6 months were overweight due to parental overfeeding.

The problem is so widespread that the British Medical Association will debate a motion on childhood obesity at its annual conference. Doctors will say that, in extreme cases, overfeeding a child under 12 should be seen as a form of abuse or neglect and treated as a child protection issue.

Dr Matthew Capehorn, who put forward the motion, said: 'If you are faced with a child who is severely under-nourished, social services, doctors and other authorities would be involved. But the same approach is not taken when faced by a child who is obese. Having a child who is overweight poses as much of a danger to their health as a child who is suffering malnutrition; arguably, even more risk.'

Dr Tabitha Randell, a consultant paediatric endocrinologist at Nottingham University Hospital, claimed some parents are killing their children with kindness. She said: 'I get many parents of obese children claiming there must be a problem with the child's glands causing the weight issues. But this is very rarely the case. Parents seem unable to accept that it is a matter of controlling food intake.'

But the Royal College of Paediatrics and Child Health does not support the conference motion. It said: 'Obesity is a public health problem, not a child protection issue.'

(Extract from www.thisislondon.co.uk, reproduced by permission of Solo Syndication)

**Document 7 Storing up problems: the medical case for a slimmer nation**

'Storing up problems: the medical case for a slimmer nation' produced jointly by the Royal College of Physicians, the Faculty of Public Health, and the Royal College of Paediatrics and Child Health, argues that action needs to be taken at every level — national, local, community and as individuals, together with an understanding of the social and cultural factors that are behind the progressive increase in overweight and obesity.

The report states that actions should be long term and sustainable, recognising that behaviour change is difficult and takes time. The emphasis is on environment, empowerment and encouragement — dropping the blame culture, engaging the whole community and assisting all groups to take action according to their own opportunities and responsibilities, including health professionals themselves.

Over half the UK population is either overweight or obese. One in five adults is obese. Obesity in 2–4-year-old children almost doubled from 1989 to 1998, and in 6–15-year-olds trebled between 1990 and 2001. If current trends continue, conservative estimates are that at least one-third of adults, one-fifth of boys and one-third of girls will be obese by 2020.

Being overweight restricts body activity, damages health and shortens life; and it harms self-esteem and social life. Heart disease, stroke, joint problems and the commonest form of diabetes (Type 2) are direct effects. Overweight and obesity also result in a huge financial burden for government, the NHS and society as a whole.

According to Professor Siân Griffiths, President of the Faculty of Public Health, the UK has the lowest physical activity for school children in Europe and we are eating the wrong foods. The solution requires partnerships at all levels, across government, who can regulate and create health policies, and within communities where engagement in healthier environments (such as schools, workplaces) can encourage individuals in making healthier choices.

(Royal College of Physicians News, 11 February 2004, www.rcplondon.ac.uk)

**3** With reference to relevant examples from documents 1, 2, 6 and 7, identify and briefly explain three factors that might affect how people react to obesity. [6]

**Answers online**

Online

### Exam summary

✔ There are likely to be several low-mark questions, for example:

- Identify several problems in defining one of the central concepts referred to in the documents.
- Identify several problems in measuring the extent of one of the central concepts referred to in the documents.
- Identify and briefly explain a number of factors that might affect how people react to the issue.

- Suggest and briefly explain problems in using a particular document to support or oppose a particular argument.
- Suggest and briefly explain problems in putting a particular policy into practice.
- State and explain one dilemma that arises in making decisions about the key issue. A dilemma is a situation where a choice must be made between mutually exclusive options, which will each result in undesirable consequences as well as benefits (see pp. 59–60).

# 7 Making ethical decisions

## Explaining how potential choices are affected by criteria

### Choices — Revised

In the examination you will be asked to consider a range of possible responses to a complex ethical problem. Various policies or courses of action will be implied or mentioned in the documents for you to identify and explore as potential choices.

Documents 1 and 2 (pp. 52–53) and 6 and 7 (pp. 55–56) suggest that responses to the problem of obesity could include:

- Take obese children into care so that their diets can be monitored daily and make it a criminal offence to allow children in one's care to become obese.
- Increase funding for research into the reasons for obesity, encouraging researchers to consult those who are obese.

**Now test yourself**

1 Suggest two responses, besides the two mentioned here, that could be made to tackle the problem of obesity. Your choices may be from the documents or reasonable ideas of your own.

Tested

### Criteria to apply — Revised

You will also be required to apply appropriate criteria to judge the effectiveness of one or more choices of action. Past questions have asked candidates to compare two choices, using two criteria, and to decide on their preferred choice. More recent questions have followed the model:

**Evaluate one choice that decision-makers might make about the problem of X. In your evaluation you should use three criteria, such as public opinion.**

You should recall from Unit 1 that a criterion is a standard, rule or test upon which a judgement or decision can be based.

Usually the question suggests one criterion as an example but expects you to work out others for yourself from the documents and your experience of the course.

**Exam tip**

OCR varies the requirements of questions over the years so seek out the most recent papers and mark schemes as models.

**Typical mistakes**

Avoid confusion. 'Criterion' is singular and 'criteria' plural.

**Now test yourself** — Tested

2 One criterion that could influence decisions about which possible policies on obesity should really be employed is 'likely effectiveness in reducing obesity'. Suggest two other criteria.

## Using the documents

While there is usually no explicit requirement to quote from the documents when applying criteria to choices, the information is there to help you and your answer is likely to be thinner and less convincing without it. You may draw on your own ideas too.

Before you start writing, reread the resources to decide which possible choices and criteria to focus on for this question. Select choices and criteria that are mentioned or implied in more than one document if possible so there is more to discuss. At the same time you could look ahead and annotate the resources in relation to credibility and plausibility, as evaluation will be required in the last question on the paper (*not* in this one).

The examiner needs to know from the start which criteria and choices you have decided to use, so it would be helpful to state this in your opening sentences and then to use subheadings to mark the stages of reasoning.

- Plan your answer so that it is coherently organised and thoughtful.
- Use separate paragraphs to apply different criteria and reach an intermediate conclusion after each.
- Show why you consider each criterion discussed is relevant and important, even though you may subsequently decide one is more crucial in reaching your conclusion.
- Explore the criteria in a balanced way. For the criterion of cost you might refer to a chart of statistics showing the high cost of a course of action. Another source, based on a medical journal, might refer to the long-term cost of *not* acting. You could weigh one against the other and conclude that, in this context, cost is not a clear criterion upon which to base a decision. The sophistication of this assessment would be rewarded.
- Consider constructing an argument so that each criterion suggests a different outcome and then give a reason why you consider one criterion more important than the other, thereby indicating the choice that should be made.
- Do not forget to reach a conclusion about the outcome of applying the criteria.
- Ensure that grammar, spelling and punctuation are very good, with few errors if any.

## Application of criteria to choices essay

Aim to demonstrate the Level 4 skills set out in the mark scheme below.

The 12 marks awarded for this question will be the sum of the following:
- A mark out of 8 for 'Application and evaluation of selected criteria to choice':
  - sound and perceptive application of the number of criteria instructed to clearly defined choice/s

- firm understanding of how criteria might support and weaken the case for the selected choices/s and/or some evaluation of criteria
- A mark out of 4 for 'Quality of argument':
  - cogent and convincing reasoning, very well structured to express and evaluate complex ideas
  - consistent use of intermediate conclusions
  - few, if any, errors of spelling, grammar and punctuation

### To aid your revision

Make a checklist of possible criteria that could be applied to courses of action relating to different situations. Some are likely to be relevant to almost every situation, such as:

- cost
- likely effectiveness
- practicality (ease of implementation)
- creation of new problems (long- and short-term side effects)

Others may apply to a narrower range of situations and appropriate phrasing may vary:

- human rights
- freedom of choice
- good of the majority
- effects on minority ethnic, religious or social groups
- effects on different age groups/sexes
- effects on wildlife/biodiversity
- effects on the environment
- effects on the workforce
- public opinion (locally or nationally)
- international opinion/likely effects on international relations

Try to add to this list yourself. If the question allows you a free choice of criteria, it can be better to avoid selecting those that are similar to ethical positions, such as 'human rights' and 'freedom of choice' (which reflects the libertarian position), as you may wish to explore these later in the final question. With this in mind, read the whole examination paper and briefly plan all your answers rather than plunging in and then realising that your answers are becoming repetitive. You are unlikely to receive much credit for making very similar points in two answers.

# Identifying dilemmas

Until recently, Unit 3 examinations asked candidates to identify **dilemmas** in the scenarios presented, and you should be prepared in case this type of short-answer question reappears.

> A **dilemma** is a situation where there are **alternative, mutually exclusive courses of action**, each of which has **undesirable consequences** for some people and **benefits for others**. In some cases the rights of a minority may have to be balanced against the wishes of the majority.

## Phrasing dilemmas

Revised

It is important to phrase a dilemma clearly and fully enough to obtain the marks available (usually 2) and the question may emphasise this by asking you to 'state and explain' a dilemma. You need to mention:

- the alternative courses of action
- the benefits of each one to people in specific situations or circumstances or perhaps to the majority
- the drawbacks of each one to particular people

Despite covering all these points, you need to avoid writing in a long and rambling way that wastes time. One way to do this is to compose two sentences beginning with the word 'if', each one dealing with a different course of action. Alternatively, the word 'whereas' or the phrase 'on the other hand' would usefully link your assessments of the two options. Here is an example of a carefully phrased dilemma.

> Enforcing harsh policies against carrying knives would probably reduce knife crime, but could criminalise craft workers who need them in their work. On the other hand, a policy where more discretion was applied could leave the public in greater danger of knife attacks.

# Supporting a choice by applying principles

The final question on the examination paper carries the most marks (36 marks in recent papers). The instructions tend to be worded like this:

**Write an argument supporting any one choice that could be made about the issue in question (a dilemma).**

**You may use the choice referred to in the previous question or any other choice.**

**In your argument you should use some relevant principles and explain why you have rejected at least one possible alternative. Support your argument by referring critically to the resource documents.**

## Ethical theories and principles

Revised

An **ethical principle** is a general rule about what constitutes right or wrong behaviour, such as 'We should treat people as equals' or 'Fairness should be a priority'. Sometimes principles are compressed to a word or short phrase, e.g. the principles of equality or fairness.

An **ethical theory** is a more developed set of moral beliefs generated by philosophers, religious groups or social movements. For example, Communists and Christians both believe in the principle that we should treat people as equals, but the groups have very different and complex theories about how and why this should be done. There are other

> An **ethical principle** is a general rule about what constitutes right or wrong behaviour. An **ethical theory** is a more complex set of moral beliefs.

important theories, such as consequentialism. The examination question gives you the choice of whether to apply ethical principles or theories or a mixture of both (even though the wording above does not make this clear), but without using some theories your answers are likely to be thin.

The question expects you to apply the principles in order to reach a decision about which is the best choice to make. Sometimes this is referred to as a **resolution** of the issue. However, it is accepted that sometimes no choice is ideal and you are expected to consider at least one alternative choice and show awareness that your eventual choice is only a partial or provisional resolution of the issue.

> Making a considered choice after applying principles is referred to as a **resolution** of the issue.

This part of the course will involve you in a certain amount of reading, checking that you understand and can apply ethical theories to a variety of situations and that you can remember them correctly.

### How many ethical theories should you know?

The specification suggests you need to know the difference between teleological (or consequentialist) theories such as utilitarianism, and deontological theories such as duty ethics. It mentions philosophers such as J. Rawls and J. S. Mill, though the earlier philosophers Kant and Bentham are similarly important. The concepts of altruism and elitism are also mentioned in the list of recommended vocabulary.

> **Exam tip**
>
> Most of your revision for Unit 3 should focus on this area.

It is advisable to be well acquainted with several ethical theories as you are expected to apply at least two and there are occasions when particular theories seem less relevant. Critical thinking writer Roy van den Brink-Budgen suggests that three theories, deontological, consequentialist and right-libertarian positions, are likely to be sufficient for dealing with most ethical dilemmas.

The account below covers considerably more. Decide which others, besides the three mentioned above, appeal to you. The natural law position, for example, is useful when considering medical and environmental ethics. You may already be acquainted with left-wing theories, Christian values or human rights from your other studies or life experience.

## Deontological versus teleological theories

Ethical theories or positions are sometimes divided into two groups:

- Those that judge actions according to whether they are well intentioned, following traditional codes of morality, regardless of their final results, are known as **deontological theories** or **duty ethics**.
- Those that judge actions according to their end result are known as **consequentialist** or **teleological** (purpose-orientated) **theories**.

A simple example illustrates the difference, although it is not always so clear cut. Suppose a loving husband were to burgle a chemist's shop because this was the only way to obtain a large supply of an expensive drug that could cure his wife's life-threatening illness.

> **Deontological theories** or **duty ethics** judge whether acts are guided by traditional moral codes, regardless of their final results. Those that focus on the end result of particular acts are known as **consequentialist** or **teleological theories**.

- From a duty ethics point of view, this action is unethical, as stealing is intrinsically wrong.
- To a consequentialist, this action could be justifiable as its purpose was to save a life and the chemist's loss is minor in comparison.

Deontological theories focus on whether acts are intrinsically good, regardless of their consequences. The word **deontological** relates to duty, doing what is obligatory or morally upright. The early Greek philosopher Socrates took this line, arguing that actions were good if they adhered to independently valid principles, but this gave rise to the question of how people would recognise and agree on these principles. An answer was suggested much later by Immanuel Kant (1724–1804).

## Kant's categorical imperative

Revised

Kant, in *Groundwork of the Metaphysic of Morals* (1783), described the **categorical imperative** — the absolute duty to follow general principles of right conduct, ignoring vested interests and possible consequences of the specific action, and acting out of **good will**. An 'imperative' is something that must be done (or in some cases must not be done) and by 'categorical' Kant meant that the moral law should be based on pure objective reason about what would be best for humankind in general, not swayed by subjective feelings about what might be the best course of action in particular circumstances. Looking up the Ten Commandments will provide guidance as to which moral rules Kant regarded as absolute.

Kant's theory is well illustrated by considering the activities of police marksmen. In 1999 an innocent member of the public, Harry Stanley, was shot dead in the street because police thought a table leg he was carrying in a bag was a shotgun. There was a long investigation after the Brazilian electrician Jean Charles de Menezes was shot in the London underground in 2005. The police who shot him thought he was a terrorist. In each case the police were focusing on the consequences of acting or failing to act. If these men had been criminals with violent intentions, then to stop them in their tracks could have saved many other lives.

In contrast, followers of Kant would say that killing is nearly always wrong regardless of the situation. Consequences can never be predicted with certainty, so it is wiser to choose actions that are intrinsically good. Even an armed villain might be talked out of his intended crime, might suddenly suffer a heart attack and be unable to carry out his plan or his bomb might fail to explode. In the cases described above it is clear that taking the deontological approach, not shooting people because it is intrinsically wrong, would have been the better of the two options.

Kant suggested that moral guidelines could be worked out using the **universalisability principle**:

People should act only in ways that they would be willing for everyone else to act in under any circumstances. Thus lying, even to save a friend, is not acceptable because all the institutions in society will crumble if we can no longer rely on each other's word.

Kant defended this position to a critic by illustrating it with a situation in which a man thought he was saving his friend from a potential murderer by trying to lie that his friend was not at home but somewhere else. Unbeknown to him, the friend had feared the attack and sought refuge in the very place named by the liar. Hence breaking a moral code is never justifiable because consequences can never be predicted. More fundamentally, it threatens to disrupt the very basis of our society. In this instance, if it was universally acceptable to lie, then no one would believe anyone and all truths would be assumed to be lies. Likewise Kant condemned laziness, suicide and unwillingness to help the needy since a universal adoption of any of these would result in social chaos.

Kant also maintained that other people should be regarded as rational beings with purposes of their own and should not be treated simply as a **means** to our own **ends**. Hence slavery is abhorrent because the master uses the slave for his own purpose with no regard for the person's rights. By the same token unfair trade and exploitation of workers are rejected by modern deontologists. Though he did not view animals as rational enough to have rights, Kant condemned animal cruelty as it lacked compassion and was likely to degenerate into unsympathetic treatment of fellow human beings. Our moral duty should be to avoid harm to others, respect their **autonomy** and be as just to them as possible.

You probably noticed the comment above that killing is '*nearly* always wrong'. Perhaps not surprisingly, as he was writing two centuries ago, Kant believed in capital punishment for murderers, following the retributive principle that criminals deserve punishment, and punishment should be equal to the harm done. Likewise robbers deserve having some of their property confiscated. Kant would almost certainly have stopped short of suggesting that those guilty of cruelty should be treated cruelly, as the dignity even of criminals has to be respected, even though they have sacrificed some of their rights to autonomy by taking away the rights of others.

**Exam tip**

Ensure that you know Kant's theory well enough to use the terms 'categorical imperative', 'good will', 'universalisability', 'means', 'ends' and 'autonomy' correctly.

**Typical mistakes**

Candidates sometimes write as if Kant were alive now, making such comments as 'Kant says it is wrong to shoot terrorists'. We can only *hypothesise* about how he would have applied his theories to modern situations.

## John Rawls and the theory of justice

Revised

The modern philosopher John Rawls followed Kant in believing that there were moral duties that should be followed for the benefit of all humanity. In *A Theory of Justice* (1971) he suggested a thought experiment. Appropriate rules of social justice could be devised if citizens representing several generations could devise the principles in advance without knowing what position they would hold in the society. This **veil of ignorance** would result in a constitution with similar rights for people of all stations and, as all had agreed to it, there should be little dispute once citizens found out the roles they were to play. Each person would have as much liberty as was compatible with that of others. The only inequalities within the society would be ones that everyone agreed were fair, so the society would be stable with little law-breaking. Of course Rawls' suggestions could be carried out to the full only if a new human settlement were to be set up, for example on another planet. Nevertheless they provide food for thought.

## W. D. Ross and conflicting duties

Ross (1877–1971) modified Kant's theory of absolute duties, suggesting that sometimes there had to be exceptions if duties conflicted. He identified several **prima facie** (at first sight) **duties** that should be obligatory unless they are overridden by other duties. In other words there is a prima facie duty to act in a certain way, unless moral considerations override this. Our **actual** duty is the duty we should perform in the particular situation. Whatever one's actual duty is, one is morally bound to perform it.

Prima facie duties are as follows:

- **fidelity** — the duty to keep one's promises and contracts and not to engage in deception
- **reparation** — the duty to make up for the injuries one has done to others
- **gratitude** — this could include providing help where possible to those who have helped us
- **non-injury** — refraining from doing others harm and making an effort to prevent harm to others from other sources
- **beneficence** — acting for the good of others to foster their health, security, wisdom, moral goodness or happiness
- **self-improvement** — to act so as to promote one's own good, i.e. one's own health, security, wisdom, moral goodness and happiness

Ross's theory is useful in that it acknowledges the importance of personal bonds in specific situations. A strict follower of Kant would be hard pressed to know whether to rescue his own loving parent or a stranger if only one could be saved. According to Ross the rescuer would be justified in prioritising the parent because of the prima facie duty of gratitude.

Unfortunately even Ross's theory has some weaknesses. He admitted that his list of duties was incomplete and did not place the duties in order of priority, making it difficult to decide which to follow if there was a conflict between them. His suggestion was that this would be self-evident to mature, intelligent people with deep moral convictions. This, however, is a rather circular argument as, if people already have this sort of moral awareness, there is no need for theories of ethics to provide guiding principles.

> **Exam tip**
>
> Learn Ross's prima facie duties as they can sometimes be easier to apply to modern situations than Kant's rules.

## Teleological or consequentialist theories

Teleological theories focus on the end results of actions, judging their morality according to the degree to which their consequences are likely to benefit or harm others. The word **teleological** is based on the Greek *telos* meaning 'goal'.

Jeremy Bentham (1748–1832) developed the consequentialist theory known as utilitarianism, in the eighteenth century. This proposed that all action should be directed towards achieving the greatest happiness for the greatest number of people. His approach was known as '**act utilitarianism**', as he attempted to calculate for a specific act various factors including:

- the number of people whose happiness would be affected
- the extent to which they would be affected
- for how long they would be affected

This was known as the **hedonic calculus** (the pleasure calculation).

Bentham treated all the people involved as equals and did not differentiate between different types of pleasure. A modern act utilitarian might justify the assassination of a ruthless dictator, which could potentially save the lives of thousands of his (or her) subjects.

Problems of adopting an act utilitarian approach include:

- Determining what all the consequences of an action are likely to be. Should we guess at the consequences for future generations?
- How we can measure and compare the different kinds of pleasure or pain various people might experience as a result of a certain act?
- Do we give equal weight to the sufferings of all, e.g. offenders and their victims?

In the nineteenth century John Stuart Mill (1806–73) in his book *Utilitarianism* modified Bentham's theory. Instead of calculating the consequences of specific acts, he suggested it was more practical to judge **types of actions**, using rules based on past experience of what would benefit society as a whole. Unlike an act utilitarian interested in the ethics of killing a ruthless dictator, a **rule utilitarian** following Mill would argue that killing leaders or people in general cannot be acceptable. Safeguarding the right to life maximises general happiness far more than condoning murder. Likewise lying and stealing are unethical because, if widespread, they result in public unease.

When considering how to act in specific situations, rule utilitarians may adopt one of two approaches:

- **Strong rule utilitarians** adhere to the general rule about what is usually beneficial, regardless of the details of this particular situation. (In this way they are likely to reach very similar judgements to followers of duty ethics, though working from a different starting point, focusing on good **consequences** rather than what is **intrinsically** right.)
- **Weak rule utilitarians** take the general rule into consideration but let the benefits and harm likely to arise from this specific act take precedence in their decision making.

Mill also differed from Bentham in distinguishing different types of pleasure. He described some types of happiness, such as intellectual pleasures, as of a higher quality than the immediate indulgence of physical desires. This went some way towards answering critics who suggested that utilitarianism might encourage pleasurable vices. For example, making alcohol free might at first glance appear justifiable as it would bring instant pleasure to many but, as it would subsequently reduce the higher quality happiness of being in good health, it would not be ethical after all.

Utilitarians argue that good actions are those that achieve the greatest happiness for the greatest number. **Act utilitarianism** entails using the **hedonic calculus** to estimate this for specific deeds.

**Rule utilitarianism** entails estimating the degree of pleasure and pain likely to result from **types of actions** such as assassinations or theft.

The contemporary philosopher Peter Singer advocates **preference utilitarianism** in his book *Practical Ethics* (1979). He argues that the preferences of all parties involved in an issue should be considered, allowing people to say what for them fulfils their interests, plans or hopes, as it can be subjective. This position may be preferable to Mill's rather elitist stance on intellectual pleasures. In addition, consideration should be given to the interests of brain-damaged people, animals and others unable to voice their views or entertain any hopes, though they may not be weighed equally against the preferences of conscious and rational people. This is a more sophisticated approach than Bentham's version of utilitarianism in which the happiness or harm to all was equally rated, though Singer's approach raises new questions about how we decide whether certain groups of people are rational enough to prioritise their preferences.

**Prudentialism** is a variation of consequentialism as it relies on predictions about the future. It is also known as the **precautionary principle**, claiming that we are entitled to act to avoid a particular negative effect. If a situation looks potentially dangerous, even though there is only a strong possibility of a negative outcome, we should take defensive steps. Prudentialists would defend the attacking of a country thought to have weapons of mass destruction before they can be used against us. Clearly Kant would take a different view, that making war is always wrong as we would not want our country to be attacked and we could never be certain in advance that the country in question was going to use weapons against us. In the case of the recent war against Iraq, the good sense of Kant's position seems clear, but in the Second World War taking a prudentialist approach against the rise of Hitler would probably have been a wiser move. A current worry is whether other nations should intervene before the 'rogue state' of Iran builds nuclear weapons.

> **Prudentialism** describes the view that it is right to take action to avert a threat.

> **Now test yourself**
>
> 3 During 2011, rulers of several states, including Libya and Yemen, sanctioned the shooting of protesters to discourage widespread rioting. How might supporters of deontological and teleological theories differ in their response to this?
>
> Tested ☐

## How much detail should you know?

Revised ☐

The developments in deontological and teleological approaches have been outlined to avoid giving the false impression that all followers of these theories have shared the views of Kant and Bentham. Some students may now feel confident enough to be able to distinguish, for example, how different types of utilitarians might try to resolve a particular dilemma.

On the other hand you may be feeling rather muddled by the fact that two theories that initially seemed diametrically opposed ended up sounding as if their followers would make similar judgements. If so, focus your revision on types of consequentialism that contrast most strongly with duty ethics. Act utilitarianism and prudentialism (the precautionary principle) are clearly very different from views such as Kant's. This is immediately clear if you consider how supporters of these theories would have justified the actions of police marksmen described earlier.

Examiners do not expect knowledge of ethical positions any more detailed than has been provided here. All you need is what you can usefully apply in the time available to the dilemma being discussed. Summaries of ethical theories without reference to the task in hand will not earn you marks.

> **Exam tip**
>
> Students finding the various types of utilitarianism confusing may want to focus on act utilitarianism if it fits the essay topic, as it contrasts well with duty ethics and can be easier to criticise than other types. Prudentialism is also straightforward to apply.

## Libertarianism

The priority of libertarians is maximum freedom for the individual to pursue his or her own goals, providing that in doing so others are not harmed. Many well-known libertarians are right wing and American, supporting capitalism and believing that the inequalities that result are inevitable. They believe those who work hard or take risks, for example by setting up businesses, deserve to be more highly rewarded than others, and for the state to attempt to redistribute wealth is misguided.

Robert Nozick, in *Anarchy, State and Utopia* (1974), objected strongly to income tax. He reasoned that some people choose to work little and enjoy more leisure. Others prefer to work longer hours, giving up their free time in order to earn more money to buy the goods they wish. Yet these people are forced through income tax to give up a portion of what they earn to the government, which redistributes it to those on low incomes, who have chosen leisure. Thus the hard workers lose out both on leisure and on money, while the idle gain both. Nozick regarded this as theft or a form of slavery, as high taxpayers work part of the week for nothing. He argued instead for a minimal state that simply keeps the peace but leaves citizens to follow their own aspirations as far as possible.

Along similar lines, Milton Friedman in *Free to Choose* (1980), co-authored with Rose Friedman, dismissed the drive to equality as unwise. He pointed out that many people object to paying income tax and, once they begin to evade that law, they could be tempted to evade others, leading to a slippery slope of law breaking. Though many sociologists argue that relative poverty leads to crime, some members of the New Right such as Friedman and Friedrich Hayek suggest that crime will always be with us, and that attempts to enhance state provision increase rather than reduce crime.

The argument is that 'welfare-ism' makes people irresponsible as they know that state benefits and social services will look after them and their dependants, so they no longer attempt to work, to save, to take responsibility for themselves or to supervise their children. Like Nozick, these New Right thinkers wish to reduce the 'nanny state' to a minimum. They advocate reducing crime by harsh deterrence, target hardening and stiff punishments rather than by redistributing wealth.

Libertarians believe in reducing the number of laws so that only acts that harm others are forbidden. So-called 'victimless offences', such as substance abuse, prostitution and viewing pornography, should not be illegal. Neither should taking personal risks, such as driving without a seatbelt. People should be encouraged to make decisions about how to conduct their own lives, and paring down the number of laws to a minimum gives individuals more practice in making mature choices as well as freeing the police to deal with crimes that harm others.

The policies of the American Libertarian Party are encapsulated in its slogan 'Smaller government, lower taxes, more freedom'. The freedoms sought include the right to take drugs, as this is a matter of personal choice and legalising it will allow police and prisons to focus on those who harm others. Restrictions on gun ownership are opposed as people have the right of self-defence. Ending the welfare system is urged because of 'its culture of dependence and hopelessness' (**www.lp.org**).

**Now test yourself**

4  What criticisms might deontologists and teleologists make of the ideas of the American Libertarian Party?

Answers on p. 105

Tested

## Paternalism

Paternalists disagree with libertarians, believing that less well-educated and immature members of the public will easily be led astray to indulge in self-harming practices unless the law acts as a deterrent. The drugs trade, prostitution and pornography involve exploitation of vulnerable people, especially the young, and are therefore not victimless. If substance abuse leads to accidents or illness, expenses are incurred by emergency and health services funded by the taxpayer and of course there are emotional as well as economic implications for victims' relatives. Despite the libertarians' desire to prioritise the freedom of the individual, many would argue that allowing people to harm themselves is neither moral nor responsible, as 'no man is an island' and what affects one affects many others. The word **paternalism** derives from the analogy that the state should be like a wise father protecting his children from endangering themselves, although those who object to this approach make a similar but more critical analogy, that of the 'nanny state' that makes us all too risk-averse and dependent.

> **Paternalism** entails supporting laws that prevent individuals from harming themselves.

## Natural Law

The Natural Law position is easy to understand, and a useful one to apply to any issue that seems to be 'going against nature', such as the creation of designer babies. This theory derived from Aristotle, who believed that everything was designed for a particular purpose and that to fulfil that purpose was natural and therefore good. The proper functions of man could be worked out by making parallels with the natural world where, for example, the purpose of a seed is to grow into a plant, and animals pair up in order to produce young. The advantage of Natural Law was that it could be applied universally, regardless of the customs of particular societies.

Thomas Aquinas built on these ideas in the thirteenth century, making Natural Law part of Catholic doctrine. God has created man and the natural world, and any acts that are not in harmony with God's purpose for us should be avoided. Hence contraception, homosexual acts and other sexual acts that cannot result in pregnancy are regarded as wrong because the purpose of sex is deemed to be the production of offspring.

This particular example reveals some of the problems of Natural Law theory. Many people would argue that sex has other purposes besides childbirth, such as emotional bonding, and that if same-sex people are drawn to each other, this must be natural. Non-religious people may dispute the whole notion of a purposeful creation. Even religious believers have difficulty in explaining the purposes of natural disasters and other aspects of human suffering. It is difficult to argue that everything that occurs naturally is for the best. While many people believe that creating GM crops is wrong because it interferes with nature too much, few would say the same about immunising children or controlling malaria-carrying mosquitoes.

The Natural Law position is still a popular one in debates about the environment, organic food, cloning, use of spare embryos created during fertility treatment, sexual selection and other bioethical controversies. In such discussions you can gain marks by pointing out the difficulties of deciding what types of behaviour are really natural.

## Human rights

Revised

Philosopher Jean-Jacques Rousseau said in his book *The Social Contract* (1762) that to live successfully alongside others in a civilised society, man had to agree to give up a certain amount of **natural liberty**, the urge to acquire whatever he could for himself by sheer power. In exchange he gained **civil liberty**, public recognition that he was entitled to keep his own acknowledged property without others interfering with it. Appointed agents of the law would defend these rights on his behalf, leaving him free to get on with other aspects of life instead of constantly having to guard his own property and safety. The term 'civil liberties' has a similar meaning to '**human rights**'.

There has been considerable debate about how binding a social contract should be, as people cannot choose the country where they are born and do not actually sign a contract. Some people advocate civil disobedience, the right to act against the law if they feel it breaches fundamental human rights. For example in 2009 protesters trespassed at Ratcliffe on Soar power station in a bid to stop it operating and thereby slow climate change. At the trial in 2011 the judge told the defendants: 'You are all decent men and women with a genuine concern for others.'

Another difficult issue is how we define **moral agents**. These are rational individuals capable of thinking about and planning actions and they are therefore held responsible for the resulting benefit or harm to others. Are children and the mentally ill or handicapped to be punished for not keeping to the social contract?

**Moral patients** are those who benefit from or are harmed by others' actions. If these are people in irreversible comas, the mentally ill or handicapped, or unborn babies, should they be viewed as having the same **moral standing** and enjoy the same human rights as rational adults? In 1990 a legal decision was made to allow a 36-year-old female inpatient at a mental hospital to be sterilised because it was deemed in her best interests by her carers, even though she did not have the mental capacity to give consent to the operation herself.

This type of debate has even extended to the rights of the dead. Dianne Blood's husband, Stephen, contracted meningitis and lapsed into a coma. Samples of his sperm were collected for later artificial insemination and he died shortly afterwards. The Human Fertilisation and Embryology Authority (HFEA) refused to give consent for Mrs Blood to use the sperm to have her husband's baby because he had not given written consent. You could make a link with Kant here, as the court was suggesting that Mr Blood was being exploited as a means to someone else's end.

However, under European law, Mrs Blood had the right to receive medical treatment in another member state, and the HFEA eventually had to let her use the sperm in a Belgian clinic. Subsequently she gave birth to two sons by this method.

A **moral agent** is someone capable of acting using moral concepts such as right and wrong. A **moral patient** is capable of benefiting from or being harmed by another's action. **Moral standing** means being considered as entitled to human rights, usually on the grounds of being a rational human being.

An ongoing debate concerns the human rights of terrorist suspects. The Habeas Corpus Act of 1679 guaranteed the citizen's right not to be imprisoned beyond a very short period without a definite charge being made, based on substantial evidence. However, terrorists could greatly endanger the public if they have to be released because it is taking too long for police to collect enough evidence against them, perhaps from abroad, and some have suggested changing the law to detain them for up to 42 days without charge. This raises the question whether the rights of a few individuals, who may be innocent, should be sacrificed for the greater safety of the rest of the population.

## International human rights agreements

Revised

Human rights are debated as part of an ongoing struggle between different pressure groups and interests. In the UK, the welfare state was founded in the mid-twentieth century based on the principle of every citizen's entitlement to certain rights 'from the cradle to the grave'. The state should supply essentials where the individual was unable to afford them and council housing, healthcare, education, income support and a range of social services were made available to the general public.

In 1948 the Universal Declaration of Human Rights was agreed by the United Nations General Assembly. This is a statement of principles that governments around the world are urged to uphold. As well as enshrining the rights to education, health, shelter and social security established by the UK welfare state, other requirements included the following:

- the right to life
- freedom from discrimination
- the right for everyone to be treated equally by the law
- privacy in the home, family and private correspondence
- freedom of expression, association and assembly (the right to gather in groups)
- freedom of thought, conscience and religion
- the right to property
- the right to vote and take part in government
- freedom from torture and cruel or degrading treatment or punishment
- freedom from arbitrary arrest or detention
- the right to a fair trial

**Exam tip**

Try to remember this list of rights as they are relevant to many contemporary dilemmas, and read more about them from websites.

They are elaborated in the European Convention of Human Rights. Look at this in some detail as the names of the rights can be quite misleading; for example, 'right to an effective remedy' is not to do with healthcare but the right to seek redress if any of one's rights has been violated. The right to the peaceful enjoyment of one's possessions is an interesting one as it can be used to protest against new developments such as wind farms or airports that might disturb local residents' peace.

We frequently hear of citizens taking their cases to the European Court of Human Rights because they are dissatisfied with how a court in their own country has dealt with an **ethical dilemma**. Sometimes they may be arguing that, by upholding the rights of an opponent, the law has deprived them of their human rights.

For more details of human rights legislation see the following and similar websites:

- Universal Declaration of Human Rights 1948:
  **www.un.org/Overview/rights.html**
- Human Rights Act 1998:
  **www.opsi.gov.uk/ACTS/acts1998/ukpga_19980042_en_1**
- European Convention on Human Rights:
  **en.wikipedia.org/wiki/European_ Convention_on_Human_Rights**

## Egalitarianism and left-wing theories

Revised

You may wish to include political theories among those you apply, especially if these are already familiar from your other studies. Egalitarians believe all people are of equal worth and should be treated the same or equally, regardless of social class, ethnicity, gender or other characteristics.

The political term **left-wing** is used to describe those whose priority is the achievement of social equality *collectively* as opposed to seeking the human rights of individuals. Moderate left-wingers, sometimes called **socialists**, believe in making gradual adjustments to achieve equality, for example by offering the poor free education, training and medical care, taxing high earners and increasing benefits to poorer people, perhaps by topping up low wages.

> **Left-wing** theories are egalitarian, seeking to extend social equality.

Marxists or Communists take a more radical line on how to bring about social equality. Karl Marx (1818–83) wrote *The Communist Manifesto* with Engels in 1847 and *Capital* in 1867 in which he described Western societies at that time as being dominated by capitalists or the bourgeoisie, wealthy owners of land and businesses. These people exploited their workers, the proletariat, and influenced them to accept this as a natural state of affairs. Marxists believe so strongly in equality that they wish to abolish capitalism, closing private businesses and putting all means of production, such as factories and land, in the hands of the state. Workers at state-run collectives would share the profits equally instead of receiving relatively poor wages from the entrepreneur owners. As capitalists would be unwilling to surrender their advantages, this could be achieved only by a revolution.

## Egoism and right-wing theories

Revised

The theories above have tended to focus on the individual's role within society, but from earliest times some philosophers have focused on the individual's duty to him- or herself. Sometimes this is accompanied by a right-wing lack of regard for the disadvantaged, as we saw in right libertarianism.

### Egoism

Ethical **egoism** maintains that each person ought to maximise his or her own long-term wellbeing. Individuals' only obligation is to pursue

> **Egoism** is the prioritising of one's own needs and ambitions.

their own self-interest. This position is not advocating self-indulgence, such as getting drunk every day, nor treating others harshly, because in the long term these actions are likely to bring negative consequences to the person concerned. Epicurus was a famous egoist who lived a simple quiet life, believing that long-term pleasure could best be obtained by contemplation of the beauty of art and ideas.

Friedrich Nietzsche, writing in the nineteenth century, stressed the need for personal development and competition, encouraging people to 'rise above the herd' and assert themselves as individuals instead of being cowed by their masters. He despised the 'slave mentality' of democracy and Christianity and asserted that 'God is dead', meaning that people should act according to their own values instead of being inhibited by a God-given morality. He argued in *Beyond Good and Evil* (1886) that 'every morality is a rationalisation of fear' and that people restrained their desires because they expected to be rewarded in the next world, whereas they should take courage and live for the moment. The *Übermensch* or superman, the person with the ability and will to throw off tradition, should pursue his own personal development according to his own values and be master of his own fate.

### Elitism

**Elitists** believe that societies need highly talented people to take the lead. There should be equal opportunities to enable all those with potential to fulfil themselves, and competition should be fair, not based on social origin. However, once selected by meritocratic processes, talented people may justifiably receive longer and more specialist training than the mass of the population and are likely to acquire more status and higher pay for their responsibilities. Elitists are likely to oppose attempts to 'reduce everyone to the same level' such as the replacement of grammar and secondary modern schools (for students who respectively passed and failed the 11 plus examination) with comprehensive schools for students of all academic abilities.

> **Elitists** are happy for some individuals to enjoy higher status conditions than others.

## Religious ethics

Revised

All religions have their own sets of ethics and some have very useful things to say about humankind's relationship with the environment, bioethics and other issues. If you are fully familiar with the views of a particular religion on an ethical dilemma identified on the examination paper, you are encouraged to discuss it, so long as you balance it with a good variety of alternative ethical positions and maintain objectivity. Most religious faiths are in line with Kant's views to a considerable extent. They advocate **altruism**, the belief that individuals should consider the good of others and act in their interests, as opposed to making their own long-term good a priority (egoism).

> **Altruists** believe that we should act for the good of others.

## Other ethical principles

Revised

In addition to the fully developed ethical theories discussed above, there are ethical principles such as fairness, need and desert, which can be applied if you have not already used them as criteria. There is generally less to say about these but referring to a relevant one might sometimes be useful to amplify an answer.

Apply principles from other subject areas such as sociology, politics, religious studies and philosophy, if they seem appropriate and you can do so confidently and objectively. Consider less-developed ethical principles, such as 'we should treat people as equal' and 'fairness'.

Look at past papers and discussions in critical thinking textbooks to see the range of dilemmas that have arisen. Then consider which ethical theories you think would be the most appropriate to apply to them and make your own notes to help you to understand and remember them.

## Critical reference to documents

Revised

The instructions to the question asking you to apply ethical principles to a choice or dilemma will instruct you to 'support your argument by referring critically to the resource documents'. This means referring to relevant information in them, accompanied by comments about the degree to which you think it can be believed. Ways you can assess the documents include the following:

- applying the CRAVEN credibility criteria to discuss whether, for example, the sources are likely to have political, religious or other biases, expertise or vested interests
- considering whether evidence is adequate, fully relevant and balanced or selective
- bearing in mind particular problems with different types of evidence, such as statistics and data from surveys
- identifying flaws in reasoning, appeals to emotion and problems with hypothetical reasoning, inconsistency and disanalogies
- recognising factors that make reasoning and evidence strong, using credibility criteria such as expertise and neutrality, and referring to positive aspects such as sample size

Try to refer to all or most of the documents to provide examples or evidence to support your answers.

> **Exam tip**
>
> Marks are allocated for referring to and assessing the documents in this question, so do not neglect this in your answer.

## Criteria for the application of principles essay

Revised

Aim to demonstrate the Level 4 skills set out in the mark scheme below.

The 36 marks awarded for this question will be the sum of the following:

- a mark out of 12 for 'Identification and application of relevant principles'
  - skilful and cogent treatment and an application of at least three principles or at least two major theories
  - clear and purposeful exposition of how the principles might be more or less useful in resolving the issue

- a mark out of 8 for 'Resolution of issue'
  - confidently expressed resolution of the stated issue on the basis of a persuasive account of the arguments on both sides
  - perhaps an awareness that the resolution is partial or provisional
  - clear and valid judgements made in coming to an attempted resolution
- a mark out of 8 for 'Use and critical assessment of resource documents'
  - perceptive, relevant and accurate use of resource material
  - sustained and confident evaluation of resource material
- a mark out of 8 for 'Quality of argument'
  - cogent and convincing reasoning
  - well developed suppositional reasoning
  - communication well suited to handling complex ideas
  - consistent use of intermediate conclusions (e.g. after applying each principle)
  - meaning clear throughout
  - frequent effective use of appropriate terminology
  - few errors, if any, in spelling, grammar and punctuation

## Planning the essay

Revised ☐

- Look through the documents again to select at least two choices that are supported by some of the evidence in the documents and by some ethical theories or principles you can write about well.
- Decide which of the two choices can better be supported by at least two ethical theories or principles. This will be your resolution of the issue.
- Think of some problem that could arise in applying at least one of the theories to the issue in question. This enables you to discuss how the principles may be more or less useful.
- Think of another principle or theory that could be used to oppose your preferred choice but support the other choice.
- Decide how you will assess the resources you intend to use. How credible and plausible are they?
- Work out the main sections of your essay.
- Using subheadings for each principle can be helpful, as can underlining each choice.

A simple plan could be as follows:

**Introduction**

Mention both choices that you intend to discuss and outline a dilemma, i.e. the benefits and drawbacks for different people if either choice were adopted. State that you intend to apply several principles to reveal which is the better choice.

## Section 1

Refer to what will eventually be your final choice (choice A) and apply an ethical theory supporting it. At this early stage in the essay it can be useful to choose a theory that could be applied in two different ways or which has obvious weaknesses, leaving the issue still rather uncertain. For example if you applied utilitarianism you might argue that the choice seems to benefit the greatest number in the short term, then counter-argue that the numbers who might be affected long term are less clear. This could involve careful hypothetical reasoning. Refer to relevant documentary evidence, concisely assessing it for plausibility and credibility. Using an intermediate conclusion, suggest that this principle has not conclusively resolved the issue.

## Section 2

As your main counter-argument, consider an alternative choice (choice B). Refer to a different theory that at first appears to support it and to undermine choice A. Use evidence to support choice B, but then try to make some negative criticism of the evidence and perhaps suggest an alternative way of applying the principle that casts doubts on the benefits of choice B. Use an intermediate conclusion to show that the issue has still not been clearly resolved.

## Section 3

Apply a third principle to your preferred choice A. You have saved until last the principle that most clearly supports your choice and undermines the alternative, together with evidence from the resources that you can assess positively as they are credible and plausible. Write an intermediate conclusion saying that this is a useful principle that unambiguously supports choice A.

## Conclusion

Conclude with an overview. Even though one principle gave some support for choice B, the evidence supporting this was weak. In contrast, two principles supported choice A and, though one was problematic, the other was very clear indeed. Choice A, therefore, appears to be a good choice to resolve the issue.

> **Exam tip**
>
> It can be useful to choose one or two ethical theories or principles that support your main choice to some extent but which are rather problematical, enabling you to argue from both sides and consider an alternative choice. Follow these with a theory that undoubtedly supports your main choice, producing a clearer resolution for your conclusion.

## What the examiner is looking for

Revised

- A thorough last essay. Candidates often run out of time. Read and plan your answers to the whole paper in order, but then consider answering early on this question and the dilemma-identifying question that precedes it, tackling the low-mark questions later. As long as you number your answers clearly, the examiner will not object to your answering questions in a different order.

- Good understanding of ethical theories. Ensure that you have read enough to be able to apply them appropriately, and that you can remember their names and key phrases such as 'universalisability'. However, do not try to show off your knowledge by describing parts of ethical theories that do not relate to the choices being made; this wastes valuable time.

- Counter-arguments in the application of each theory. These may arise when the principle is applied to different groups of people mentioned in the documents. Alternatively, you may discuss how different philosophers' application of the theory, such as act versus rule utilitarianism or Kant and Ross's versions of duty ethics, could result in a different conclusion.

- Explanation of the relevance of each principle you apply to the dilemma.

- An essay organised into paragraphs. You may also want to use subheadings for each principle and for your conclusion.

- Use of most of the documents as evidence at some point in the essay.

- Assessment of the sources of documents and the credibility and plausibility of their evidence. Demonstrate your knowledge by using specialist terminology such as 'expertise' and 'argument by analogy'.

- Hypothetical reasoning, using phrases such as 'If...then...might happen'.

- Each section in which you have applied a principle rounded off with an intermediate conclusion assessing its usefulness in resolving the dilemma.

- Completion of the essay with your assessment of which ethical principle was the most useful, acknowledging any difficulties that might arise in resolving the dilemma.

- Correct spellings of frequently used words such as 'criterion', 'principle' and 'deontological'. Try to allow time to check over your work for errors of spelling, punctuation and grammar.

## Check your understanding

Tested

1 What is meant by an ethical principle?
2 Explain the meaning of ethical dilemma.
3 Explain what is meant by applying criteria to resolve an issue.
4 Give another name for deontological theories.
5 What term did Kant use for the concept that we should regard an act as right only if we were willing for everyone to do it?
6 Explain Kant's idea about using people as means to an end.
7 What did Kant mean by the categorical imperative?
8 What was meant by Rawls' veil of ignorance?
9 Which philosopher suggested a list of prima facie duties that might help people faced with conflicting duties?
10 What is meant by a teleological theory?
11 Explain Bentham's idea of the hedonic calculus.
12 How does act utilitarianism differ from rule utilitarianism?
13 What is meant by prudentialism?
14 What did Jean-Jacques Rousseau mean by the 'social contract'?
15 Which human right was enshrined in the Habeas Corpus Act of 1679?
16 What are the attitudes of libertarians to laws and taxes?
17 What is the connection between paternalists and 'the nanny state'?
18 How does altruism differ from egoism?

Answers on p. 105

## Exam practice

**1** Suppose you had selected 'taking obese children into care so that their diets can be monitored daily and make it a criminal offence to allow children in one's care to become obese' as your choice for a question reading as follows:

**Evaluate one choice that could be made to address the problem of obesity. In your evaluation you should use three criteria (such as cost).** [12]

Allow yourself 15 minutes to reread and annotate documents 1 and 2 (pp. 52–53) and 6 and 7 (pp. 55–56) and then time yourself to see whether it takes you much more than the 15 minutes or so available to write your response.

**2** Read the passage below and then make a detailed essay plan for the following question:

Write an argument supporting either banning the creation of test tube 'designer babies' as saviour siblings or allowing parents to use this procedure.

- In your argument you should use some relevant principles or ethical theories and explain why you have rejected the alternative choice.

- In your answer, discuss the relevance of three of the ethical theories summarised above, refer to details from the document and remember to reach a conclusion.

**'Designer baby' gives hope to his ill brother**

**A couple banned from creating a test tube 'designer baby' in Britain to help cure their seriously ill 4-year-old son have had a baby boy after treatment in America. Jamie Whitaker was selected from nine embryos to be the best possible tissue match for his brother Charlie. His parents hope to use stem cells from his umbilical cord to treat Charlie's life-threatening blood disease.**

**Jamie is only the second British baby to undergo 'tissue typing' tests as an embryo. Yesterday's announcement triggered a debate over the ethics of screening embryos for desirable traits, and how far the state should interfere with parental choice. Charlie suffers from diamond blackfan anaemia, a rare blood disorder in which bone marrow produces too few red blood cells. The only cure is a transplant of bone marrow stem cells from a donor with the same immune system cells. Neither of Jamie's parents nor his sister were suitable.**

**A naturally conceived sibling has a one-in-four chance of being a match. After giving birth to Emily, the couple wanted to improve the chances by screening embryos created by IVF. Mr Whitaker said: 'We have always wanted four children, so we just combined having more with helping Charlie.' Blood tests over the next few days will reveal whether he is a perfect tissue match. There is a one in 50 chance that Jamie will carry the same disease as his brother.**

**Psychologists have argued that babies born to provide tissue to transplant may resent their siblings later in life. Jack Scarisbrick, of the anti-abortion charity Life, said: 'It is wrong that of nine human beings created, eight have died. There has been a huge deliberate wastage of human life. No doubt this boy will be very much loved but children should be brought into the world unconditionally and not to serve some other purpose.'**

(Extract from '"Designer baby" gives hope to his ill brother' by David Derbyshire, *Daily Telegraph*, 20 June 2003, www.telegraph.co.uk, reproduced by permission of Telegraph Media Group Ltd 2003)

**3** For practice, read the documents below and plan an answer to the question, ideally developing this as an essay for your teacher to mark.

Write an argument supporting any one choice that the government could make concerning the fortification of flour with folic acid to improve the nation's health. In your argument you should use some relevant principles and say why you have rejected at least one alternative choice. Support your argument by referring critically to material from the resource documents. [36]

**Document 1 Folic acid in bread to cut birth defects**

**Folic acid will be added to bread within a year to reduce the number of babies born with spina bifida and other defects. It will be the first time since the Second World War that food manufacturers have been ordered to add nutrients to improve the nation's health. Experts believe that the compulsory addition of folic acid will reduce the number of cases of spina bifida and other defects by 40%. The vitamin also reduces miscarriages and may help to combat strokes, heart disease and bone disorders in adults.**

**The decision will raise concerns from some consumers at the erosion of personal freedoms. Compulsory addition of folic acid was ruled out by the Food Standards Agency 4 years ago because medical experts feared that it would mask a vitamin deficiency in the elderly. However, adding folic acid will lessen the 200 cases of babies born each year with spina bifida or other neural tube defects. It will also relieve the**

distress of up to 750 women a year who have an abortion after discovering that their baby may be born with neural tube defects.

The Agency's advisory committee estimates that if flour were fortified with folic acid at levels of between 100 and 450 micrograms per 100 grams, the number of pregnancies affected by neural tube defects would fall by between 40 and 370 a year. The committee said it now favours compulsory addition of folic acid provided that GPs can monitor the scale of B12 deficiency in elderly patients. Lack of it can trigger anaemia and damage to the nervous system.

Women thinking of becoming pregnant are already advised to take folic acid supplements and to eat foods such as broccoli, Brussels sprouts, beans and peas, which are rich in the vitamin. But half of all pregnancies are unplanned, and the women most at risk are those from poor income groups who are less likely to take vitamins out of ignorance or forgetfulness.

(Extract from 'Folic acid in bread to cut birth defects' by Valerie Elliott, *The Times*, 5 April 2006, www.timesonline.co.uk)

**Document 2 Folic acid might help to combat Alzheimer's**

The risk of developing Alzheimer's might be lowered by the consumption of a higher level of folic acid through diet and supplements. Researchers at Columbia University Medical Centre looked over 6 years at the diet and progress of 965 healthy people who had an average age of 75. Around one in five, 192, developed Alzheimer's disease — but those with the highest intake of folic acid had the lowest risk. The recommended daily dose of folic acid is 400 micrograms (0.4 mg) but the average intake in the UK is around 0.2 mg.

Dr Jose Luchsinger, who led the study, cautioned: 'The findings of this study are in contrast to those of some other research. The decision to increase folate intake to prevent Alzheimer's disease should await clinical trials.' Dementia affects over 700,000 Britons, with 500 new cases diagnosed every day as more people live longer.

(Extract from 'Folic acid might help to combat Alzheimer's' by Jenny Hope, *Daily Mail*, 8 January 2007, www.dailymail.co.uk, reproduced by permission of Solo Syndication)

**Document 3 Breast cancer fear for pregnant women over folic acid tablets**

Taking large amounts of folic acid during pregnancy may increase the risk of breast cancer, a study has suggested. The finding will alarm many women, who are advised by the Department of Health to take folate tablets to protect against having a baby with spina bifida. Doctors were quick to reassure women yesterday, saying that the study results could be a chance finding, were not statistically significant and applied to levels of folate much higher than those recommended by the Department of Health.

The new data comes from the long-term follow-up of nearly 3,000 women who took part in a trial of folate supplementation in 1966–67. They were divided into three groups and given either 5 mg or 0.2 mg folate tablets or a placebo. A team led by Dr Andy Ness of Bristol University has followed up the women nearly 30 years later. In the British Medical Journal, they report that 210 of the women have died over this period, and that more of those taking folate, especially at the higher rate, have died than those who took the placebo. The strongest links were seen for breast cancer, where death rates for those on 5 mg folate were twice as high as those on placebo. There were, however, only six deaths in this category, which means that the results are not statistically significant.

In a commentary in the British Medical Journal, two US doctors say that other evidence suggests that folate supplementation reduces the risks of breast cancer, especially in women who drink alcohol. Godfrey Oakley and Jack Mandel say that the finding should not deter the fortification of flour with folic acid, which has reduced both birth defects and deaths from heart attacks and strokes in the US.

(Extract from 'Breast cancer fear for pregnant women over folic acid tablets' by Nigel Hawkes, *The Times*, 10 December 2004, www.timesonline.co.uk)

**Document 4 Institute of Food Research, news release**

'Fortifying UK flour with folic acid would reduce the incidence of neural tube defects', said Dr Siân Astley of the Institute of Food Research. 'However, with doses of half the amount being proposed for fortification in the UK, the liver becomes saturated and unmetabolised folic acid floats around the blood stream.

'This can cause problems for people being treated for leukaemia and arthritis, women being treated for ectopic pregnancies, men with a family history of bowel cancer, people with blocked arteries being treated with a stent and elderly people with poor vitamin B status. For women undergoing in-vitro fertilisation, it can also increase the likelihood of conceiving multiple embryos, with all the associated risks for the mother and babies.

'It could take 20 years for any potential harmful effects of unmetabolised folic acid to become apparent.'

It has already been shown that folic acid fortification can exhibit Jekyll and Hyde characteristics, providing protection in some people while causing harm to others. For example, studies have confirmed that unmetabolised folic acid accelerates cognitive decline in the elderly with low vitamin B12 status, while those with normal vitamin B12 status may be protected against cognitive impairment. Around 20% of over 65s in the UK have low B12 status.

Similarly, dietary folates have a protective effect against cancer, but folic acid supplementation may increase the incidence of bowel cancer. It may also increase the incidence of breast cancer in postmenopausal women.

Dr Astley suggests that the use of folic acid in fortification even at low doses could lead to over-consumption of folic acid with its inherent risks.

(www.ifr.ac.uk)

### Answers and Unit 3 quick quiz online

## Exam summary

- Unit 3 is a synoptic paper. It tests all the skills you developed during AS (AO1, AO2 and AO3) but in a less compartmentalised way. Quality of written communication is assessed under AO3.

- Unlike the AS papers, there will be no ruled spaces under the questions for your answers. You will need to write in the general type of examination answer book, in black ink. As this gives you no guidance on how much to write for particular questions, time yourself when you do practice papers to see what you can realistically achieve. As well as the question paper there will be a resource booklet of documents.

- You should be able to evaluate a wider range of more challenging, genuine source material than the brief documents written specially for the AS examination. The maximum length is likely to be 1,250 words. These provide background to an exercise in selecting choices of action according to certain criteria and then applying ethical theories and principles to an ethical dilemma. From the documents you need to select appropriate ideas and information to support your reasoning and analysis.

- You need to identify and evaluate conflicting ideas and arguments within the source material, and explain how they may be influenced by a range of factors such as political or moral views of the writers. Apply the credibility criteria covered in Unit 1 to discuss how seriously the sources should be taken in the decision-making process.

- The evidence and reasoning in the documents also needs to be assessed in terms of its strengths and weaknesses, bearing in mind what you learnt in Units 1 and 2 about adequacy, relevance, problems

with different types of evidence, such as statistics and data from surveys, flaws in reasoning, appeals to emotion and problems with hypothetical reasoning.

- There is likely to be a question worth about 12 marks asking you to apply several criteria to evaluate one or more choices that could be made to resolve an issue.

- You need to show awareness that there may be a range of possible responses to complex moral and ethical problems, such as introducing new legislation, changes in administration, arousing public awareness or taking no action.

- The question paper may suggest some criteria for you to discuss, but you will need to work others out for yourself from the documents and your own experience.

- Explain why each criterion is relevant and important, e.g. why public opinion matters in decision making.

- Try to show how particular criteria can sometimes work in different ways, both supporting and undermining a particular choice, e.g. a scheme might be expensive in wage bills but have the effect of saving the NHS money, making the criterion of cost a difficult one to apply.

- Support your points with information from several of the documents.

- Organise your response in paragraphs, each ending with an intermediate conclusion assessing the usefulness of the criterion just applied in making the choice under discussion.

- Subheadings relating to the different criteria or choices may help to guide the reader.

- Remember to write a conclusion stating which choice you support and the criteria that have been most useful in reaching this decision.

- The last question is likely to be worth 36 marks, asking you to write an argument supporting a choice and explaining why you have rejected at least one alternative choice.

- In your argument identify and apply relevant principles, which may be derived from ethical theories.

- Take at least two ethical theories or three principles or a combination in turn and discuss how supporters of these positions would be likely to view the choices.

- Your answer should be supported with material from the resource booklet, using as many documents as are relevant and critically assessing them as you do so.

- You are not expected to have detailed theoretical knowledge of ethical theories and principles and will not be rewarded for summarising them without making their relevance clear. However, you should be able to apply named ethical theories.

- Your answer must be a coherent essay examining alternatives in the form of argument, sustained counter-argument and suppositional reasoning, assessing the likely consequences of alternative courses of action.

- Use subheaded paragraphs when applying each principle and end them with intermediate conclusions assessing the principle's usefulness.

- Use specialist terminology such as rights, means, end, entitlement, deserts, deontological, consequentialist, elitist and altruistic.

- Ensure that you do full justice to a range of possible views, resisting the temptation to oversimplify issues. Finally, even though by its very nature a dilemma can never be fully resolved, conclude by identifying the ethical theory or principle that suggests the most satisfactory resolution, and explain your choice.

# 8 Analysis

Unit 4 is a synoptic paper. It relies on knowledge and skills developed at AS and you may, in writing your own argument, be able to refer to ethical theories learnt in Unit 3.

Unit 4 resembles Unit 2 in the skills required, but needs a greater level of sophistication and some additional knowledge. (It differs in that Unit 4 has no multiple-choice questions.) You are required to:

- analyse parts of a passage, identifying its components and their functions (AO1)
- evaluate an argument, identifying weaknesses and strengths (AO2)
- write your own argument in response to the passage (AO3)

## Familiar elements of arguments

### Revising the components of argument — Revised

Begin by revising the components or elements of argument from the AS specification and its standard notations. Write the words in full where no established abbreviation applies, as in the case of claim. You need to be able to recognise and write about the functions in a particular context of the following:

- argument
- claim or assertion
- main conclusion (C)
- reason (R)
- evidence (Ev)
- example (Ex)
- intermediate conclusion (IC)
- counter-argument (CA) consisting of counter-conclusion and counter-reason

- counter-claim or counter-assertion
- counter-example
- explanation
- argument indicator
- assumption (A)
- principle (P)
- hypothetical or suppositional reasoning (HR)
- analogy (Ag)

> **Exam tip**
>
> Do not invent your own abbreviations. Think what confusion would arise if you chose C for claim and Ex for explanation.

### Counter-assertion, counter-claim or counter-argument? — Revised

Some AS textbooks may treat counter-assertions, counter-claims and counter-arguments as if they are the same thing, in order to simplify matters. By A2 you should know the difference. 'Assertion' and 'claim' are different words for the same element but 'argument' has a different meaning, and the same applies to the words associated with these terms.

- An assertion or claim draws a conclusion without giving reasons.
- An argument consists of conclusion plus reason(s).

- A counter-assertion or counter-claim opposes an argument without giving reasons.
- A counter-argument opposes an argument, giving reasons. It comprises a counter-conclusion and a counter-reason.

## Response to counter-assertion or counter-argument — Revised

A reason that directly challenges a counter-assertion or counter-argument is known as a **response** or sometimes a **challenge**. At AS it is usual to categorise these together with reasons supporting the main argument, but their function is slightly different. They tend to follow straight after the counter-argument, weakening it before the arguer goes on to give reasons supporting the main argument.

> A **response** or **challenge** undermines a counter-argument or counter-claim.

In an argument against flying because of its environmental impact, an example of a counter-assertion or counter-claim plus response is as follows:

> **Some people think that flying to holiday destinations is acceptable (counterclaim), but they should try to find alternative means of transport (response to counterclaim).**

An example of a counter-argument plus response is as follows:

> **Some people think that flying to holiday destinations is acceptable (counter-conclusion), because the planes are going there anyway (counter-reason) but the public should realise that by choosing alternative means of transport and thereby reducing demand they could help to protect the environment (response to counter-argument).**

In this second example, because the reason for the opposing statement is provided in the counter-argument, there is more for the challenger to argue with, so the response tends to be more substantial.

# Less familiar elements of arguments

## Scene setting — Revised

This refers to explanatory background material that often precedes an argument. A newspaper article may begin by providing basic facts about an event or trend before supplying an argument about what action should be taken. You may be required to distinguish the argument from the scene setting.

## Now test yourself — Tested

1 Distinguish the scene setting from the argument in the following and identify the conclusion of the argument:

   **The cleric described as Osama bin Laden's helper was released on bail yesterday, despite the Prime Minister's vows to protect the public against terror. Clearly there needs to be a change in the law that currently makes it impossible for us to deport dangerous people who may not receive a fair trial in their own countries. Few countries have such a fair legal system as ours, so this reasoning means we could be stuck with countless foreign offenders. This excessive concern for the underdog presents an unnecessary risk to our own population.**

## Rhetorical devices

These are means of gaining and keeping the interest of the audience or reader. They are rarely part of the reasoning itself, but add to the emotional impact of the argument. Consider this extract from a speech by Barack Obama when campaigning for President. It is very persuasive, yet it contains little that could be described as reasons or evidence. Most of it is rhetoric.

> Years from now, you'll look back and you'll say that this was the moment, this was the place where America remembered what it means to hope. For many months we've been teased, even derided, for talking about hope. But we always knew hope is not blind optimism. It's not ignoring the enormity of the task ahead or the roadblocks that stand in our path. It's not sitting on the sidelines or shirking from a fight. Hope is that thing inside us that insists, despite all the evidence to the contrary, that something better awaits us if we have the courage to reach for it, and to work for it, and to fight for it.

### Rhetorical question

This is a question intended for dramatic effect, not to draw an answer. An example is 'Who would be so mean as to refuse to help these poor people?'

### Repetition

Martin Luther King made substantial use of this device:

> Let freedom ring from Lookout Mountain of Tennessee! Let freedom ring from every hill and molehill of Mississippi. From every mountainside, let freedom ring.

### Hyperbole

This is the use of excessive, often exaggerated language designed to stir the audience or reader, for example when Martin Luther King said:

> I have a dream that one day even the state of Mississippi, a state sweltering with the heat of injustice, sweltering with the heat of oppression, will be transformed into an oasis of freedom and justice.

## Appeals

Appeals to emotions such as fear, hatred or sympathy are a type of rhetorical device, trying to persuade the reader to accept the conclusion. A charity encouraging the public to sponsor children in developing countries includes in its publicity material the rhetorical question 'Imagine changing the life of a child like Elsy?', accompanied by an attractive photograph. Appeals may help to carry the argument by influencing the reader's emotions rather than by providing logical reasons to support the conclusion.

## Rant

Rant is an emotional assertion of opinion. It may consist of claims supported by no reasons at all or by appeals or irrelevant reasons. Rant may appear on the surface to be argument but it is not.

## Strands of reasoning

This refers to the various groups of arguments and counter-arguments that constitute a longer argument. The arguer may pursue various lines of thought in different paragraphs, each time providing several reasons to support an intermediate conclusion. One strand of reasoning might support an intermediate conclusion by extended analogy and another by developed hypothetical reasoning.

## Move

Revised

A move is a switch from one strand of reasoning to another, implying that there is some connection between them. For example, the writer might reveal a UK problem in one strand of reasoning and then move to describing the way a supposedly similar problem has been dealt with abroad. You might be asked to evaluate how effective this move is.

## Independent and joint reasons and chains of reasoning

Revised

A conclusion may be supported by one reason or several. **Independent** or side-by-side **reasons** may make the argument more persuasive by their accumulative effect, but the conclusion could still be reached if supported by only one of them. Here is an example:

> You should visit the Tutankhamun exhibition in London because the treasures on display are said to be the most spectacular archaeological finds anywhere in the world and you will need something interesting to do in the school holidays.

**Independent reasons** work individually to support a conclusion. **Joint reasons** work only in conjunction with others.

In this case you could imagine the arguer adding more independent reasons, such as special price offers, to induce the listener to visit the exhibition.

In contrast, **joint reasons** work together to support the conclusion, as in the following example:

> You should visit the Tutankhamun exhibition in London because the treasures are not going to be on display in any other European city and you are unlikely to be able to afford to visit them when they return to Egypt.

Here, if either of the reasons was absent, the conclusion would not be reached. It is only the combination of the unavailability of the treasures in Europe and the prohibitive cost of seeing them in Egypt that makes the argument persuasive. Joint reasons work together as a series of steps, and three or more reasons working in this way are known as a chain of reasoning.

## Sustained suppositional reasoning

Revised

Suppositional argument means exploring one or more **suppositions** or imaginary scenarios in order to think more clearly about a situation and solve a problem or decide upon a course of action. Nigel Warburton provides a good example of a brief piece of suppositional reasoning in *Thinking from A to Z* (1996):

> Supposition: A premise assumed for the sake of argument but not necessarily believed: sometimes known as a presupposition. Suppositions, unlike assertions, are not presumed to be true: rather they are instrumental in finding out what is true.

For example, a police inspector might say the following: 'Let's suppose the murderer did enter the house by the window. Surely we'd expect to find some evidence of forced entry.' The inspector is not asserting that the murderer definitely did enter the house; nor even that that is probably what happened. The inspector is inviting us to follow through a chain of reasoning based on the supposition that the murderer came in through the window. In other words, the inspector is offering a hypothesis about what might have happened.

If Warburton had provided the complete chain of reasoning, revealing whether there was evidence of forced entry and what it might mean, this could have been developed into sustained suppositional reasoning.

# Using skills of analysis

There have been various types of analysis question on the Unit 4 paper:

- a series of 2-mark questions quoting short sections from a passage, with instructions
- analysing a section of the argument in detail
- assessing whether a document is an argument
- analysing the extent to which a document supports a claim

## 2-mark questions                                                    Revised ☐

**Name the following elements and briefly explain their function in the structure of the reasoning.**

Naming the component correctly earns 1 mark, and relating it briefly to other parts of the argument to show its function earns the second mark. A recent exam had the following 2-mark answers:

- This is a reason to support the conclusion that 'I don't think this surveillance is such a big deal'.
- This is a response to the counter-assertion that 'you may find all this surveillance rather chilling'.

In contrast, the answer

- Response to counter-assertion

gained only 1 mark.

> **Typical mistakes**
>
> Candidates sometimes identify a component without explaining its function in the argument. Even for a main conclusion, mention how it is drawn from quoted intermediate conclusions.

## Analysing a section of the argument in detail                       Revised ☐

Instructions could be as follows:

**Analyse in detail the structure of the reasoning in paragraph X by identifying elements of the reasoning (such as reasons, intermediate conclusions etc.) and showing their relationships to each other.**

To tackle this question:

- Write out phrases or sentences from the passage in the form of a list, indicating what components they are by using standard abbreviations (R1, R2, IC1, IC2 etc.).

- Add verbal explanation where necessary to identify scene setting, independent or joint reasons and other features.
- Refer to elements that play a role in the argument but do not appear on the page, such as assumptions working as reasons to support the argument, writing them out in your own words.
  - Similarly the writer may challenge an **imagined** counter-argument with a response such as

    Yes, it's extreme but we have to do it.

  - If analysing such a passage you would write out the missing part of the argument and identify it, together with the visible parts of the argument, e.g.

    This measure is too extreme — anticipated counter-assertion

    'Yes, it's extreme but we have to do it' — response to anticipated counter-assertion

- Your verbal account may be accompanied by a diagram clarifying the structure of the argument using notations.
- Because the articles for analysis have not been written with the examination in mind, differences of opinion may arise when identifying some components. If you have alternative answers for some components, write down both, explaining concisely your thinking. Well-justified answers will be credited, even where there is some variation.

> **Exam tip**
>
> Read the key paragraphs more than once before writing down your analysis, as you may change your mind after closer scrutiny. Remember to include assumptions.

## Assessing whether a document is an argument    Revised

This question, worth about 4 marks, will ask you to justify your decision whether the article is an argument. A top-level answer should make about 4 points, supported by quotations, such as:

It is an argument because it has a conclusion (quoted).

This is supported by intermediate conclusions such as (quoted), supported by reasons such as (quoted), backed by evidence such as (quoted).

It responds to the counter-argument in paragraph X.

However, the argument does not begin until paragraph Y, as the preceding section is scene-setting.

It is unlikely that a long document will *not* be an argument, as it would make other questions hard to set. However, it is possible that only part of it may be an argument, or you may be able to argue that it is not a true argument as the reasoning supports a slightly different conclusion. If a shorter passage, such as a blog, is set for this question, it may well be a rant as opposed to an argument.

## Analysing the extent to which a document supports a claim    Revised

Instructions could be as follows:

**To what extent does the author of document 1 support claim X and on what grounds? Justify your answer with reference to**

**his reasoning (e.g. his conclusions, reasons, assumptions and/or implications).**

It is essential to remember that this question, worth about 14 marks, comes under the heading 'Analyse' so this is what you should do. Evaluation of arguments will be required in the next section of the paper.

The question is really asking you to distinguish parts of the argument supporting a particular claim from parts arguing in the other direction. To prepare your answer:

- Look at the conclusion, to see whether it is in favour of or opposed to the claim.

- Check your impression by reading the document carefully again, looking at the reasoning to be sure whether it is the main argument or the counter-argument that supports the claim mentioned.

- If the main argument supports the claim, analyse the document by highlighting the conclusion, intermediate conclusions, reasons and evidence supporting the reasons, using different colours to clarify your thoughts.

- If, on the other hand, the counter-argument supports the claim, mark the counter-arguments and counter-claims, identifying counter-reasons, counter-conclusions and any supporting evidence.

- Check whether there are any hidden components that support the claim, such as assumptions or implications.

- Now write up your answer. Begin by stating whether the main conclusion is for or against the claim. Then identify the components that support the claim. To avoid very long quotations, it may sometimes be possible to refer to paragraphs, for example by saying that paragraph 2 begins with the first reason supporting the claim and in the second sentence provides two pieces of evidence supporting the reason.

- A thorough answer should include identification of parts of the argument that support the opposing view and perhaps a reference to parts of the document that do not support the claim because they have another role, such as scene setting.

2 Decide whether the following passage is an argument, giving reasons.
   **People all over the world have been interested by the pro-democracy demonstrations in North Africa and the Middle East. Hundreds of innocent people as well as protesters have been killed in Libya and Bahrain, so some wonder whether other countries should intervene to help the rebels. If Western powers do become involved, it may be said that our goal is not democracy but to control the oil these nations produce.**

Answers on p. 106

## Check your understanding

1 What name is given to the background information often supplied before an argument begins?
2 What is meant by rhetoric or a rhetorical device?
3 What is hyperbole?
4 What is rant?
5 What is a strand of reasoning?
6 What is a move in argument?
7 How do independent and joint reasons differ?
8 Explain what suppositional reasoning is.

Answers on p. 106

## Exam practice

Read this challenging article by Janet Street-Porter and answer the questions that follow. Bear in mind there are 'hidden' parts of the argument. If you have alternative answers for some components, state this and explain your reasoning.

**A return to the ration book is the answer to obesity**

1 **A whopping number of kids — around a quarter — are now officially overweight before they've even started primary school, according to new statistics released by the Department of Health. It has only taken a couple of generations for small children to morph from skinny live wires into chubby couch potatoes who sit glued to their screens, don't walk anywhere and who shun the idea of sporting activity.**

2 **When I look back at pictures of me as a child, I look skeletal by today's standards — in 2008 any mum with small children the size we were back in the 1950s would be hauled before a child protection agency and accused of starving her offspring.**

3 **The fact is, my parents went through rationing during and after the war, and were thinner because they ate much less meat and protein, exercised more and, even though money was short, ate more fresh food and far less processed muck.**

4 **Now we've got more money and allegedly a higher standard of living, but no sense of when to stop eating. And don't tell me it's about poverty — if a third of the nation's 11-year-olds are overweight before they start secondary school, it's a disease that affects all classes and income levels.**

5 **The government is waffling about inspecting lunch boxes — an idea that will never work. What we need is dead simple. Bring back rationing. Don't talk to me about human rights — at this rate one third of the younger generation aren't going to make it past 50 before they peg out from heart failure.**

6 **Evil fatty processed foods should be strictly rationed with government stamps and ration books. We should be limited to strict quotas of meat per person per week, allowed unlimited fresh fruit and vegetables. Sugar, chocolate, fats, salt should only be available with coupons. Yes, it's drastic — but look where free choice has got us.**

(Janet Street-Porter and *Independent on Sunday*, 24 February 2008)

1 Identify and briefly explain the function of the following elements in the structure of Street-Porter's argument:

   a 'A whopping number of kids — around a quarter — are now officially overweight before they've even started primary school, according to new statistics released by the Department of Health.' (paragraph 1) [2]

   b 'The fact is, my parents went through rationing during and after the war, and were thinner because they ate much less meat and protein, exercised more and, even though money was short, ate more fresh food and far less processed muck.' (paragraph 3) [2]

   c 'Evil fatty processed foods should be strictly rationed with government stamps and ration books.' (paragraph 6) [2]

   d 'Yes, it's drastic' (paragraph 6) [2]

   e 'but look where free choice has got us' (paragraph 6) [2]

2 Analyse in detail the structure of the reasoning in paragraphs 4 and 5. [12]

**Answers online**

## Exam summary

- Unit 4 is worth 60 marks and 25% of the total A-level. It is a synoptic paper and relies on the knowledge and skills developed at AS. Each section carries 20 marks, so divide your time about equally between the three sections.

- The passage is likely to be a genuine article from the media, written for an educated audience.

- It will not be a simply structured argument but one with several developed strands of reasoning.

- There are likely to be several low-mark questions quoting phrases from the passage and asking you to identify and briefly explain their function in the passage.

- You may be asked to analyse the structure of a whole paragraph or strand of reasoning in detail. You can make use of diagrams and recognised notations to clarify this.

- You should include assumptions and anticipated counter-claims at appropriate points of the argument, even though these are not a visible part of it.

- You may have to decide whether a passage is an argument and explain your answer.

- As well as elements of argument studied in Units 1 and 2, you will be expected to recognise and explain the function of the following:
  - scene setting
  - joint or independent reasons
  - multiple intermediate conclusions
  - developed counter-arguments
  - suppositional or hypothetical reasoning
  - rhetorical devices
  - rant

# 9 Evaluation

## Evaluation at A2

AS refresher ──────────────────────────────── Revised ☐

Begin by reminding yourself of the strengths and weaknesses in reasoning and evidence covered in Units 1 and 2, including the definitions of specific flaws and why they constitute poor reasoning. Any of these could be encountered in Unit 4 passages but they will not be flagged up for your attention as before. Instead of being asked to name particular flaws or evaluate reasoning in specific paragraphs, you will be presented with a whole passage and asked to evaluate the reasoning as a whole, identifying some of the strengths and weaknesses that you view as significant.

Evaluating assumptions ──────────────────────── Revised ☐

You may need to identify and assess assumptions when evaluating the quality of reasoning in an argument. This is likely to involve:

● judging whether or not they are reasonable assumptions

● stating whether what is assumed is a fact that can easily be established, one that would be difficult to investigate or an opinion or principle that people might disagree about

● evaluating the extent to which the strand of argument, and perhaps the whole argument, is weakened if the assumption is not justified

Evaluating analogies ──────────────────────── Revised ☐

At A2 you will need to notice for yourself analogies embedded in a passage, rather than being directed towards them. You will need to evaluate whether the analogy is an apt one and assess whether its use strengthens or weakens the reasoning in that strand of the argument.

## Deductive reasoning

The study of valid and invalid forms of argument is a new element of Unit 4. Most of the arguments you will have encountered so far are **inductive**, ones where reasoning leads us to suppose there is a high probability that the claim is true, but there could always be a slight element of doubt. Conclusions in the social sciences arise from studies of a sample of people considered to be sufficiently large and representative. Induction is therefore based on an accumulation of evidence, leading to a conclusion that is highly **probable**. However, it would be wrong to describe these conclusions as 'proved'.

In contrast, **deductive reasoning** involves a logical working out of a conclusion, rather like in mathematics. The conclusions are **certainly** true if the reasons are true and the structure of the argument is **valid**.

## Valid deductions

There are two valid forms of hypothetical argument, which are quite easy to recognise. They are usually expressed in the form of two sentences, each of which has two parts. The first sentence (the premise) has the familiar 'if A then B' structure:

> **If Jon gets three grade As at A-level, he will be accepted by Oxford University.**

The first part of this sentence is called the antecedent and the second part is the consequent.

The second sentence draws the conclusion:

> **Jon has obtained three grade As, so he will be accepted by Oxford University.**

This form of argument is known as **affirming the antecedent**, because conditions set in the first part of the first sentence have been achieved. Providing the first statement is true, the second must logically follow. This valid structure is also known as *modus ponens*.

**Denying the consequent**, also known as *modus tollens*, is another valid structure:

> **If Jon gets three grade As at A-level, he will be accepted by Oxford University.**
>
> **I have just heard that Jon was not accepted by Oxford, so he can't have got his three As.**

In this case it is the consequent that has not been achieved, so we can deduce the required conditions were not met.

## Formal fallacies

Revised

Unfortunately there are two patterns of argument that look similar to those above but which are not valid. The premises can be true without the conclusions being true. They are known as formal fallacies because their form is misleading. They are as follows:

### Affirming the consequent

> If Jon gets three grade As at A-level, he will be accepted by Oxford University.
>
> Jon has been accepted by Oxford, so he must have got his three As.

This is not necessarily true. The premise was not that Jon would be accepted *only* if he got three As. Sometimes universities accept students who just fail to meet their conditions, especially if they impress in some other way, such as taking critical thinking as a fourth A-level!

Unit 4 Critical Reasoning    91

## Denying the antecedent

> If Jon gets three grade As at A-level, he will be accepted by Oxford University.
>
> Jon has not managed to get three As, so he won't be accepted by Oxford University.

In this structure the second sentence begins with a negative form of the antecedent of the first sentence. The conclusion may turn out to be true but it is not certain, for the same reason given above. The admissions tutor may be generous.

### Now test yourself                                         Tested ☐

1   Consider the following. Identify the form of deductive argument and decide whether the conclusion must be true.

**Ben's father said he could go on holiday to Greece with his friends if he passed all his GCSEs. He's just been booking a Greek holiday so he must have passed them all.**

Answers on p. 106

### Syllogisms                                               Revised ☐

This is another form of deductive argument, with two premises followed by a conclusion. Each part contains a different combination of two of the three terms mentioned in the argument. A valid form of the syllogism has the following simple structure:

> All As are B.
>
> C is A.
>
> Therefore C is B.

Its structure guarantees that the conclusion must be true if both premises are true. A simple example is as follows:

> All mammals are warm-blooded.
>
> Rats are mammals.
>
> Therefore rats must have warm blood.

People are sometimes misled by an argument that closely resembles this form, known as the **fallacy of the undistributed middle**.

> All mammals are warm-blooded.
>
> Birds are warm-blooded.
>
> So birds must be mammals.

The difference begins in the form of the second premise. The argument runs as follows:

> All As are B.
>
> C is B.
>
> Therefore C is A.

This fallacy gets its name from the term that occurs in both premises, in this case warm-bloodedness. It is undistributed because its use does not apply exclusively either to mammals or to birds, so it cannot be used to argue that birds and mammals are the same.

It is easy to see how people can make the undistributed middle error. Here is another example:

Students (A) get concessions at the cinema (B).

That old lady (C) has just obtained a cheap ticket (B).

She (C) must be a student (A).

While this could be so, it is more likely that the old lady got a pensioner's concession. Concessions at the cinema are not confined to students; they apply to retired people and cinema staff as well.

This structure closely resembles the examples above of the deductively invalid form affirming the consequent.

The rules concerning syllogisms can be confusing and in fact examples of deductive arguments occur only rarely in Unit 4 passages. If you are faced with a confusing argument structured like a syllogism, it can be helpful mentally to change some of the parts to examples you find easy to think about. Always bear in mind that the initial premise may be a sweeping generalisation, in which case the conclusion may be unsound, regardless of the precise form of the argument.

## False converse

Revised

Changing round the key terms of a two-part statement produces its converse. People sometimes think that the converse of a true conditional proposition will also be true, but this is often not the case. Assume that the true statement is as follows:

If it is raining, then the school fete will be cancelled.

Now consider the converse:

If the school fete is cancelled, then it will be raining.

This is not necessarily the case because the fete might be cancelled for other reasons, such as lack of support.

## Law of excluded middle versus fuzzy logic

Revised

Having looked briefly at logic, we ought to bear in mind its limitations too. According to classical logic, for any given statement and the negation of that statement, if one is true, the other must be false.

More recently philosophers have become interested in **subjectivity**, the notion that propositions might be possible but uncertain and that there could be degrees of truth or middle ground. This is known as **fuzzy logic**. You can see its relevance if you consider the statements: *David Cameron is a good Prime Minister* and *David Cameron is not a good Prime Minister*. Many people would tend to agree to some extent with both statements for different reasons.

# Evaluating appeals

Revise the appeals covered in the AS course: appeals to popularity, history, tradition and such emotions as pity and hatred. These rhetorical means of persuasion are often regarded as weaknesses in argument as they employ loaded words such as 'terrorists', 'victim' and 'brutality' to arouse the feelings of the reader rather than providing sound evidence. However, emotional appeals can contribute to the force of an argument if used together with logical reasoning and compelling evidence. An appeal to fear can be valid if it is accompanied by truthful evidence of what may happen if precautions are not taken.

'Beware! Touching this hotplate could cause serious burns' does arouse emotions in the reader but they reinforce an important message, the truth of which could easily be tested.

In contrast, Enoch Powell's famous 'rivers of blood' speech about curbing immigration to Britain contained many appeals to fear that were not backed by sound reasoning and evidence. For example, the prediction that Powell quoted from a member of the public, 'In this country in 15 or 20 years' time the black man will have the whip hand over the white man', had the capacity to arouse fear and hatred without providing any evidence to support it. The phrase 'whip hand' was particularly emotive, as it conjured up the image of blacks enslaving whites. The fact that the prediction was made in 1968 about a Britain two decades into the future makes it demonstrably clear that this was a misleading appeal to emotion.

## Appeal to authority
Revised ☐

These require careful evaluation. An arguer may quote from the Bible or the Qur'an or refer to a well-known precedent to add weight to his or her argument. Although appeals to inappropriate or unnamed authorities constitute weaknesses in reasoning, an appeal to a relevant authority, especially where there is no evidence of disagreement from other authority figures, may strengthen an argument.

You can read more about appeals on the following website:
**www.skeptics.org.uk/forum/showthread.php?t=446**

## Evaluating a single argument
Revised ☐

Sometimes an examination question requires you to evaluate one argument. It might ask how effectively the author supports the conclusion.

- The passage has not been deliberately written to contain flaws, so it may take time to identify any weaknesses and they may be fairly subtle, although some should fall into familiar categories such as assumption, sweeping generalisation, inconsistency, or inadequate evidence.

- Read through the passage carefully and underline in pencil any points that strike you as possible strengths or weaknesses. In the case of weaknesses, decide which are important enough to affect the overall credibility and plausibility of the article and write about these rather than minor quibbles.

- Try to make a variety of points, for example by referring to single examples of different named flaws as opposed to multiple examples of the same flaw.

- Think of a precise way to describe the argument's strengths, which we tend to take for granted. The CRAVEN criteria may be helpful.

- Remember to consider rhetorical devices such as loaded language and appeals, which can be seen as flaws if not backed by reasoned argument and convincing evidence.

- As well as examining the precise content of the article, note any important issues that should have been considered but have been neglected, as this will enable you to reach a holistic judgement about the effectiveness of the argument.

- Before you begin to write, organise your points logically, grouping the strengths and weaknesses or working chronologically through the article.

- You are not expected to discuss every possible strength and weakness in the article and indeed some questions specifically remind you to be 'selective'. Calculate how much time you should spend on this question and do not overrun; the evaluation section as a whole carries a third of the examination marks.

- After examining specific strengths and weaknesses, weigh up your overall impression, providing a holistic evaluation.

> **Typical mistakes**
>
> Candidates often spend too long on this section, leaving insufficient time for the last question.

## Evaluating moves

Revised

Sometimes questions invite you to evaluate an author's move from one part of the argument to the other. The article by Janet Street-Porter (p. 88) is shorter than a typical examination piece so the number of moves is limited. However, you should still be able to identify that there is a move from observing that children in the past used to be thinner to predicting that the current generation of children is in danger of dying by 50. This is followed by the move proposing rationing. Evaluating moves means discussing whether they follow logically and convincingly from each other. To do this:

- Make a selection of points about specific strengths or weaknesses in the author's reasoning in her move from one claim to the next.

- Include an overall assessment of how convincing and logical the move is. In the model answer below, this assessment comes first.

  Street-Porter's move from observing that children in the past used to be thinner to her prediction that 'one third of the younger generation aren't going to make it past 50' is problematical as the reasoning is flawed in two respects.

  She takes it for granted that being 'officially overweight' is less healthy than being 'skeletal'. Despite mentioning the Department of Health she supplies no scientific evidence of the dangers of being 'officially overweight'. Though it could be assumed that readers will already be convinced by this, it is obesity that is most frequently associated with high risk. Of the 'third of the nation's 11-year-olds [who] are overweight', a much smaller proportion will be obese and some will only be marginally overweight.

Furthermore her projection into the future does not allow for the possibility that anti-obesity campaigns may be effective in persuading today's 11-year-olds to adopt healthier lifestyles as they mature.

## Evaluating a linked passage

Revised

Another type of question provides a second passage in which a different author has either responded to the first article or independently expressed an alternative view. You could be asked to evaluate the second argument as it stands or to assess how effectively it counters the first. Here is the response of a blogger to the Street-Porter article:

> **Do you really want to cut childhood obesity? Start a war. This will ensure that more women stay at home to look after the kids and cook them proper food. People will respect their elders. And supply routes for food will be cut.**
>
> (www.independent.co.uk/opinion/commentators/
> michael-williams-readers-editor-790220.html, reproduced
> by permission of *Independent*)

This response is a straw person, as the blogger has picked up Street-Porter's reference to one apparently beneficial aspect of war, rationing, and expanded upon it to suggest, tongue in cheek, that we should start a war to achieve conditions that would reduce people's weight.

Alternatively, it could be described as a **reductio ad absurdum** since a ridiculous outcome is derived by appearing to accept Street-Porter's suggestions that lifestyles were better in wartime.

The blogger's response is really rant. It is weak on two counts. First, there is no reasoned argument seriously addressing any of the issues raised by Street-Porter or suggesting alternative solutions. Second, what Street-Porter has said is distorted, as she does not explicitly blame obesity on lack of home cooking and makes no reference at all to lack of respect for elders, a complete irrelevance. The response is amusing but lacks coherent reasoning and is therefore ineffective in countering Street-Porter's article.

> **Exam tip**
>
> If asked to evaluate a longer passage as a response to another, it is useful to underline the parts of the second argument that contradict or refer to points made by the first, to help you organise your answer.

## Comparing two passages

Revised

One question found in recent examinations has been along the following lines:

**Is the reasoning stronger in document 1 or document 2? Justify your answer with selective reference to key strengths and weaknesses in each document and their effect on the strength of the reasoning.**

To tackle this question:

● Read each document carefully, seeking strengths as well as weaknesses in each and underlining them.

● Focus on the way specific claims are supported and the effect this has on the overall reasoning.

- Decide whether to assess one document and then the other, comparing them at the end, or to switch frequently between them, comparing them in a number of ways as you go. The latter is more sophisticated but some candidates find it confusing.

- Ensure that you conclude with a holistic judgement that follows from your observations and is not overdrawn.

Another question type is as follows:

**Discuss the extent to which document 2 counters document 1. You should come to a reasoned judgement.**

Remember that this question, worth about 20 marks, comes under the heading 'Evaluate'. It is not to be confused with the 'Analyse' question mentioned earlier ('To what extent does the author of document 1 support claim X and on what grounds?').

This time you need to look closely at the content of the two arguments. It is likely that they disagree to some extent, but in quite subtle ways, perhaps with some common ground. Your task is to summarise accurately the reasoning in each, using your own words to show understanding but with supportive quotation. As you do so, compare them, drawing attention to points of conflict and points of agreement. Remember to reach a final judgement about how strongly they disagree.

## Check your understanding

Tested

1 How does deductive reasoning differ from inductive?
2 In hypothetical deductive reasoning, what is meant by the antecedent of the premise?
3 What is meant by the consequent of the premise?
4 What is another phrase for *modus ponens*?
5 Is denying the consequent a valid form of reasoning or a formal fallacy?
6 What name is given to a type of deductive reasoning such as 'All As are B; C is A, therefore C is B'?
7 Does an appeal to authority strengthen reasoning?

Answers on p. 106

## Exam practice

1 Turn again to the Janet Street-Porter article (p. 88) and answer the following:

How effectively does Street-Porter support the claim in the article's title that 'a return to the ration book is the answer to obesity'? [20]

2 Is the reasoning stronger in Street-Porter's argument (p. 88) or in Gard's argument below? Justify your answer with selective reference to key strengths and weaknesses in each document and their effect on the strength of the reasoning. [20]

**We should never lose sight of the fact that Western populations are, by and large, as healthy as they have ever been. We might also remember that there is a large body of opinion to the effect that one of the greatest threats to Western economic prosperity is our ageing population. While there are some that say we are about to see life expectancies nose dive, the majority of demographic opinion sees life expectancy continuing to rise. It is impossible for both points of view to be correct.**

**These complexities should direct us towards a focus on people's health and the quality of their lives as opposed to their body weight. Rather than making policies and laws that indiscriminately target everyone, we should be identifying those groups for whom access to physical activity and high-quality**

food is a problem. We know that people will use the streets for exercise if they think they are safe. We know that people who are poor and working multiple low-paid jobs will use junk food because it is cheap and convenient.

There is no all-encompassing obesity crisis but there are always areas of public health which are worthy of concerted attention. The past tells us that, if preventative public health is to be our goal, focussing on the material conditions of people's lives rather than hectoring, blaming and shaming them is more likely to achieve results.

(Extract from *Obesity and Public Policy: Thinking Clearly and Treading Carefully*, Dr Michael Gard, Charles Sturt University)

**Answers online**

Online

## Exam summary

✔ You will be expected to evaluate the support given to a claim over several paragraphs or one or two whole documents. This will require a carefully planned and structured essay.

✔ As well as identifying flaws and strengths studied in Units 1 and 2, including making use of credibility criteria, you should be able to recognise the following and comment on their effects on the reasoning:

- deductively valid argument structures such as affirming the antecedent (*modus ponens*) and denying the consequent (*modus tollens*)
- formal fallacies, affirming the consequent and denying the antecedent
- syllogisms
- fallacy of the undistributed middle
- false converse
- appeals

- other rhetorical devices such as rhetorical questions and loaded language
- More detailed assessment of analogies and hypothetical reasoning may be needed.

✔ Any assumptions will need to be identified and assessed.

✔ You may be asked to evaluate moves from one strand of the argument to another.

✔ There could be a question asking you to compare the strengths and weaknesses of two arguments, deciding which is the stronger, or to assess the effectiveness of one as a response to the other.

✔ You might need to discuss the extent to which one document counters the other and come to a reasoned judgement.

✔ Remember to take a holistic overview of any passage being evaluated, assessing its development through the various strands to its conclusion.

# 10 Writing your own argument

## Approaching the task

Writing your own argument at A2 is more demanding than at AS, so you need to get plenty of practice and feedback from your teacher.

### How to tackle the topic
Revised

The topics set tend to be quite abstract, asking candidates to write their own arguments supporting or challenging the claims, such as:

**Freedom is meaningless without safety.**

**Technological change should be welcomed.**

**Equality is an unattainable dream.**

**The end can never justify the means.**

The issues above are similar to those you encountered when discussing ethical dilemmas in Unit 3 and you should bring similar skills to bear, considering the complexity and ambiguity of terms such as 'freedom', 'technological change' and 'equality'. Your argument could include an attempt to define a key term and you might qualify your conclusion depending on how the term is interpreted.

Some of the reasons you include could be based on ethical theories such as utilitarianism or moral principles, and you could cite an alternative ethical theory as a counter-argument. This would produce a sophisticated answer and demonstrate a sound synoptic understanding of the whole course. (Nevertheless there is no requirement to mention ethical positions.)

Spend some time thinking widely about the issue, as you will not be credited for repetition of any of the arguments or evidence in the passage. For example, the passage accompanying the essay title 'Equality is an unattainable dream' was entirely about feminism but the question invites more of an overview. It is unlikely that a candidate whose argument focused exclusively on feminism would score as well as one who included examples and evidence about other equality issues, such as class, race and disability, though there would be no harm in making some references to feminism that were very different from those in the passage. A sophisticated candidate might differentiate between equality of access or opportunity in the eyes of the law, and fully realised equality of achievement, which is much harder to obtain.

### What the examiner is looking for
Revised

To score top level marks your argument should:
- be a response to the precise title set, not a slightly different topic
- have a title indicating whether it supports or challenges the claim

- be based on your own ideas, not those in the original documents
- include discussion of ambiguous or complex terms in the question, perhaps qualifying conclusions reached depending on their interpretation
- be planned and carefully structured to include several strands of reasoning supporting a number of intermediate conclusions — there should be several reasons in each strand, most of them supported by examples and evidence
- include a developed counter-argument recognising contrasting points of view and identifying the reasoning underpinning them, before challenging them effectively with a thorough response
- use analogies, sustained hypothetical reasoning and principles if appropriate
- have a conclusion that is clearly stated, despite being in the title as well, and which is well supported by all the reasoning
- be persuasive: this means selecting appropriate issues you are reasonably informed about and ensuring that your reasons are relevant and adequate, not making exaggerated claims of the sort encountered in slippery slope arguments. Evidence and examples must be convincing, avoiding references to imaginary research. Avoid relying on dubious assumptions.
- prioritise quality over quantity: a carefully organised, convincing and sophisticated argument of 300 words is likely to be more highly rewarded than a rambling argument of twice the length. A recent OCR marking scheme commented, 'Candidates will not have time to produce thorough arguments covering all possible strands of reasoning and responding to all counter-arguments. We should reward candidates who have demonstrated the ability to argue cogently, coherently and concisely. We are looking for an intelligent, thoughtful, structured response.'
- be written in a formal register using mature vocabulary. Check your work for errors of spelling, grammar and punctuation, as these aspects of communication are assessed. OCR advises: 'We want to credit language which means something and which is clear, succinct and precise. We want to credit communication of good thinking. We do not want to over-reward flowery or waffly language which says very little.' This means avoiding rhetorical questions and other rhetorical features such as appeals, dramatic repetition and loaded language.

## Exam practice

Janet Street-Porter comments: 'Look where free choice has got us.' Write your own argument to support or challenge the claim that allowing the public free choice of lifestyle is harmful. [20]

**Answers and Unit 4 quick quiz online**

Online

## Exam summary

- ✔ Unit 4 is worth 60 marks, which represents 25% of the total A-level marks. Questions are grouped under the headings 'Analyse', 'Evaluate' and 'Develop your own reasoning'. You have to answer all questions, some of which require short answers and some essays.

- ✔ The exam is allocated 1 hour 30 minutes. Take care to reserve time for your own argument.

- ✔ You write in the general type of examination answer book, which gives no guidance on how much to write for particular questions, so time yourself on practice papers to see what you can realistically achieve. Divide your time about equally as the three sections carry 20 marks each.

- ✔ When writing an argument of about 300 words challenging or supporting the claim provided (usually of an abstract nature):

- ● Avoid using the same reasons and evidence as the passage. Your essay can refer to different topic areas providing it still fits the claim.

- ● Use your Unit 3 experience to discuss ambiguous words in the claim and use ethical theories in your own argument if you wish.

- ● Plan the structure carefully, providing several strands of reasoning including a developed counter-argument and several intermediate conclusions. Examples and evidence must be persuasive, with only a few reasonable assumptions being required. Additional elements such as analogies and sustained hypothetical reasoning are welcomed.

- ● Use formal and accurate language avoiding rhetoric, emotional appeals and waffle.

# Answers

## 1 The language of reasoning

### Now test yourself

1 The second sentence is the reason that supports the conclusion stated in the first sentence. If you are unsure, apply the *therefore* test. Try the conclusion indicator word *therefore* or *so* and then the reason indicator word *because* between the two sentences, to see which fits the context.

'Critical thinking must be a good test of intelligence *because* our students' grades relate closely to their IQ scores.'

Clearly *because* fits well, whereas *therefore* makes no sense, confirming the second sentence as the reason.

2 The first sentence is the main conclusion, supported by the reason in the second. The third sentence, defending school sports, is the counter-argument. The counter-conclusion is 'Some defend school sports', supported by counter-reasons 'exercise counteracts obesity and strengthens the bones of the young'. The next sentence is a reason challenging the counter-argument, signalled by the indicator *however*. The argument is completed by another reason supporting the main conclusion.

3 The first sentence is the conclusion. The two reasons supporting it are the following broad points:

- A man's sense of responsibility for his child tends to be weakened if he feels excluded straight after the birth.
- Fathers often lack information about caring for babies, which they could easily learn from the hospital staff.

The sentences following each of these reasons are supporting evidence, in each case from an informed source.

4 Though this outcome seems likely, it is only conjecturing about a possibility. In such a condition, some men might still take little responsibility for their own children. The argument is weak because we cannot predict the future with certainty.

5 There are several assumptions including:

- My son still enjoys chocolate.
- He has not reduced his previous consumption of chocolate for health reasons.
- He will not already have been overwhelmed with Easter eggs from other people.
- Going out to buy Easter eggs is preferable to ordering them online.

6 Views collected from *Daily Mirror* readers are unlikely to reflect the full range of attitudes you could expect from a national poll. The sample is likely to be of predominantly lower social classes and less educated people, so it is not representative of British people.

7 A representative sample is made up of a variety of respondents with all the significant different characteristics of the relevant population in the same ratio.

Valid data reflect a true picture of the situation being studied; for example the respondents are motivated to tell the full truth.

8 The mode is the most common score in a series, the mean is the average and the median mark is the middle score.

The mode gives little idea of how the class as a whole performed. The mean can be skewed by a few exceptional marks and may take longer to calculate than the median, which gives a fair impression of average performance. Revealing the range rather than the median may be more upsetting to the student with the lowest score, because the median does not reveal the lowest score.

### Check your understanding

1 An argument attempts to persuade whereas an explanation gives a reason for a phenomenon without attempting to persuade; the explanation may be already generally accepted among people knowledgeable in the relevant field.

2 Counter-conclusion and counter-reason.

3 'Therefore' and 'so'.

4 Evidence is often based upon research, consisting of qualitative or quantitative data or expert views, and it provides broad support to reasons. Examples provide illustrative support to the reasons, using specific instances that may or may not be typical.

5 An element.

6 You should not attempt to rephrase the component. Neither should you try to save time by just copying out the beginning and end of the component with dots in between (ellipsis). Another fault would be to copy out more than the component, e.g. by including an example embedded in a reason.

7 An unstated part of the argument that is necessary in order for the conclusion to be reached.

8 Assumptions are not written down in the argument.

9 Hypothetical reasoning speculates about the outcome that is likely to arise if a particular future condition is fulfilled or it may conjecture about how the past might have been different if a particular condition had been different.

10 The reason may be irrelevant, inadequate or unreasonable (implausible) or may not be significant enough if conflicting reasons are stronger.

## 2 Credibility

### Now test yourself

1 Galliano would have a vested interest to lie about the incident as expressing racial hatred is a punishable offence, whereas his accuser has no known vested interest to fabricate the story. The video evidence constitutes 'ability to perceive'. Racist behaviour in the videoed incident would be consistent with similar behaviour towards the art historian.

2 C = corroboration or consistency

R = reputation of the individual or the group he or she belongs to

A = ability to perceive, such as eyewitness or camera evidence

V = vested interest, where the source has something to lose or gain from his or her testimony

E = expertise or experience of a relevant nature

N = neutrality, where the source has no bias

## Check your understanding

1 A way of deciding whether or not a source is believable.

2 With vested interest an individual or source has something to lose or gain for his or her own benefit. Biased individuals may be swayed because of affiliations with a particular group. In other words, they may be inclined to distort the truth to support another party, not necessarily for their own benefit.

3 'Ability to perceive' is a broad term that incorporates other senses such as hearing and the use of mechanical aids such as video cameras, whereas 'ability to see' suggests eyewitnesses only.

4 Hearsay is information that has been passed on by word of mouth and may, consequently, be inaccurate.

5 Plausibility means likely or reasonable, based on the reasoning and evidence provided and common sense.

## 3 Analysis of argument

### Now test yourself

1 People who are very similar tend to be attracted to each other (R1).

However, when we know someone is a relative, our strong incest taboo normally makes us resist any attraction to him or her (R2).

It is therefore important that people know who their close relatives are (IC).

Occasionally siblings are brought up apart, without knowing who their biological parents are (R3),

as in the recent case of the twins parted at birth who married each other and later found out their true identities (Ex).

People who adopt children must ensure that they are informed about their biological parents as early as possible (C).

2 (a) The principle could be phrased as 'The police should protect public freedoms' or 'A democracy should prioritise people's civil rights'. Do not include a reference to imprisonment without trial as this is too specific for a general principle.

Upholding this principle entails fair treatment by the criminal justice system. This appears to be undermined by imprisoning suspects indefinitely without charge because insufficient evidence is available. (It contravenes habeas corpus, the traditional right to be charged with a named offence so that it is possible to organise a defence and have a fair trial.)

(b) A counter-argument might reason that, by taking those suspected of trying to harm the public off the streets, the police are upholding one of the principles of a liberal democracy. This is that the law-abiding majority should be free to go about their own business in safety.

3 The first definition is the more appropriate. In contrast, the second definition fits the word's use in the first sentence of the passage.

### Check your understanding

1 An interim conclusion reached part way through an argument. An intermediate conclusion is supported by reasons and in turn supports the main conclusion.

2 She gave the persistent tramp a couple of socks as his feet were bare.

*or*

She gave the persistent tramp a couple of socks on the jaw and he staggered off in pain.

## 4 Evaluating arguments

### Now test yourself

1 This is a flawed argument at various stages. Not all students will use their loans so foolishly and some may find well-paid jobs swiftly and be able to repay the loans. Mortgage companies take loans into account but will sometimes lend to those whose earnings make it feasible for them to pay the loans off gradually. Not everyone would be depressed by being unable to buy their own home and most depression does not lead to suicide.

2 There are at least two emotional appeals in this extract, an appeal to anger in the first sentence and an appeal to pity or horror in the second.

3 Statistics may be affected by changes in the overall population and may not be sensitive enough to reveal important factors, for example failing to distinguish between more girls committing crime and more crimes by a small number of girls. They may also be affected by factors such as greater public willingness to report certain offences and increased activity by professionals in response to new initiatives such as target setting. (Notice that under-age drinking was the only factor mentioned in the article that could help to explain a genuine increase in the proportion of girls committing crime.)

4 Answer (b) is precise enough to merit 2 marks. Answer (a) is far too general, as animals are not being likened to people in any other way than the one just stated, as potential bearers of disease. 1 mark would be generous.

5 Possibilities are as follows:
- Only the really committed are getting married now, as cohabitation has become more acceptable, so those marriages that do take place are more likely to last.
- A higher proportion than formerly of those who choose to marry have a religious faith, as others see no moral objections to cohabiting. Those who have made vows before God will be reluctant to break them and some may see divorce as a sin.
- The trend has increased to marry at an older age, reducing the length of marriages and thus the likelihood of divorce.
- The economic problems of recent years may make couples increasingly reluctant to split as it is more expensive to live in separate homes.

Note: the decline in the numbers marrying is not a sound explanation, as the rate of divorce is a proportion of those marrying, not a raw number of divorces. Always take care to distinguish between a rate and a number.

6 (a) is an example of sound logical reasoning of the suppositional kind. The cautious wording 'would be likely' leaves open the possibility of reconsidering an unusual case of disease A if necessary. (b) Hypothesising about events

that did not occur in the past is weak reasoning as it is pure speculation that could never be proved or disproved. In fact, there could be any number of reasons why no world war has occurred in the last half century, including the founding of the United Nations and the collapse of the USSR.

7 The general principle is not applicable if people wish to stir up racial hatred and there are a number of laws restricting what can be said on matters of defence. The BBC has policies of maintaining a balance of moderate opinion and excluding extreme views likely to offend. You might also have thought of situations where there is a rule of silence, such as in examinations.

## Check your understanding

1 A post hoc flaw arises when someone thinks that, because one event is followed by another, the first has caused the second. Correlation equals cause confusion relates to trends rather than single events. Here the false conclusion is drawn that because there is a correlation between patterns of events, for example the increase in women doing paid work and the increase in child crime over the same period, one has caused the other.

2 In *tu quoque* the accused person says that the person making the accusation or someone else has committed the same offence and so has no right to object. In 'two wrongs' the accused person says that the accuser or other people have committed a different but comparable offence.

3 A necessary condition is a requirement for something to be achieved, but it may not be the sole requirement. A sufficient condition is the sole requirement in order to achieve the goal.

4 A hasty generalisation is based upon limited experience of something, perhaps a single instance. A sweeping generalisation is usually based upon the view that all members of a group conform to a stereotype.

5 *Ad hominem*. He accused them of an irrelevant attribute and therefore did not consider their views.

6 Restricted options or choices.

7 No two historical events are similar in every way, so acting in the same way will not necessarily have the same results.

8 An appeal to tradition.

9 Appeal to popularity.

10 An analogy that is inappropriate. The situations being compared differ in significant ways.

11 A conclusion is overdrawn if it is based on inadequate reasons. A more limited conclusion would be better supported by the reasons.

12 An example or instance that supports the counter-argument.

## 5 Developing your own arguments

### Now test yourself

1 The resulting argument could emerge as follows, though this model is probably longer than you have managed in 15 minutes. Ask a teacher to mark your attempt at this task.

### An argument supporting the view that education should be made compulsory to the age of 18

There has been some opposition to the raising of the school leaving age to 18 because many young people dislike school (CA). However, there has been opposition to every attempt to extend education since 1870, however beneficial (R1).

Most students usually develop the independent study skills needed for later life after their mid-teens (R2). Research suggests that in the early secondary years they regard their teachers as the main source of knowledge and it is not until later that they begin to think for themselves (Ev). Furthermore, young people need to learn not only facts but about abstract matters relating to adult life (R3) such as current affairs, ethics and other life and leisure skills (Ex). Psychologists suggest abstract reasoning is best accomplished in the later teens (Ev). So continuing education to 18 is essential for young people's self-development as independent learners fully prepared for the adult world (IC1).

An extra 2 years at school could provide students with additional vocational skills needed in the modern workplace (R4), particularly computing and less familiar languages such as Mandarin and Arabic (Ex). Social skills, such as learning to solve problems effectively in teams, would teach them to work effectively with others (R5 and Ex). Therefore extending education would benefit the economy by better preparing young people for work (IC2). Thus there are compelling reasons why education should be made compulsory to the age of 18 (C).

## Check your understanding

1 Weaknesses in arguments include:
- reaching a slightly different conclusion from the one provided
- failing to structure the argument clearly using all the components required
- attempting to support the conclusion with reasons and evidence that are in the original passage
- making up evidence that is unconvincing
- writing in an inappropriate style, for example using frequent rhetorical questions

## 6 Answering the short questions

### Now test yourself

1 Civil rights supporters prioritise freedom of expression and religious belief and freedom from surveillance and persecution as well as freedom from imprisonment, whereas to a prison officer the term would mainly suggest the state of not being imprisoned. The differences arise because civil rights supporters campaign for a broad range of human rights whereas the prison officer's profession is centred around the physical reality of incarcerating and releasing offenders.

## Check your understanding

1 The 'conclusion' of a concert always means the end, whereas the 'conclusion' of an argument refers to the final stage

of the reasoning, though it may not be placed at the end. The problem arises because the word is used differently in different contexts. The first usage is an everyday one and the second a specialist, academic usage.

2   Cultural relativism refers to the way people from different backgrounds may have different ideas about what is right and wrong. In some countries animals are viewed just in terms of their usefulness and it is customary, for example, to overload pack animals such as donkeys, with no regard to their suffering. At the opposite extreme, Buddhists regard all life as equally valuable and are reluctant to kill even 'vermin'. In Britain it would be regarded as abuse to beat children and to expect them to do long hours of work, whereas in many developing countries child labour is accepted.

## 7 Answering the longer questions

### Now test yourself

1   Two responses could be drawn from the following:
- Focus on informing the public about the unhealthy properties and effects of some foods on sale.
- Make lessons on healthy eating and cookery compulsory in schools and ask schools and workplaces to promote walking and other exercise.
- Send experts regularly to the homes of obese children to give dietary advice.
- Take no action at all to tackle obesity itself but campaign to reduce the problem of stigma.

2   Possible answers include:
- effects on public expenditure
- human rights
- creation of other problems

3   Supporters of deontological ethical positions would definitely regard the shooting of protesters as wrong because killing is absolutely wrong. Teleological theories might justify it if the consequence were to prevent widespread rioting with huge loss of life, fear, turmoil and damage to property, though these days most people would emphasise the human rights of the individual protesters too.

4   Deontologists would support the welfare system, arguing that it is our duty to support those unable to fend for themselves. Applying Kant's principle, we might not wish allowing others, especially the inexperienced and vulnerable, to harm themselves by taking dangerous drugs to be universally applied. Certainly deontologists would not approve of carrying weapons, as the only motive for this must be to harm others if the situation arises.

Most teleologists would probably argue that removing all welfare benefits would cause great hardship to the elderly, ill and vulnerable, doing more harm than good, and therefore they would oppose it. Likewise teleologists would worry that allowing widespread drug use and gun ownership would be likely to increase addiction, ill health and violence. If it could be proved that permitting these would reduce crime, as libertarians argue, but would still increase ill health in addicts, it would be hard to reach a decision using the hedonic calculus.

### Check your understanding

1   An ethical principle is a guideline or broad statement about what constitutes right or wrong. It may be developed into a fuller ethical theory.

2   An ethical dilemma is a situation in which, whatever choice is made, there are likely to be unfortunate consequences as well as good ones.

3   Resolving an issue means making a decision in an attempt to solve a problem. This can be done by considering various choices in the light of criteria or factors such as fairness or cost.

4   Duty ethics.

5   The principle of universalisability.

6   All human beings have a right to autonomy, to lead their own lives independently and achieve their own ends. It is wrong for us to use others as a means to our own ends, for example to exploit them through slavery.

7   The categorical imperative is the absolute duty to follow general principles of right behaviour in all situations, regardless of possible consequences.

8   Rawls believed that, if people could decide on the rules of a society, without knowing what position they would hold in it themselves, they would arrive at a system that was as fair as it possibly could be.

9   W. D. Ross.

10  Also known as consequentialism, it bases decisions about what is right on the likely effects of actions in particular circumstances.

11  Bentham tried to calculate the amount of pleasure or pain likely to arise from particular acts by considering a number of factors such as the numbers of people affected, how intensely and for how long.

12  Act utilitarianism looks at a specific situation and judges right action according to the pleasure or pain caused. Rule utilitarianism considers the likely effects on the public of types of actions and decides whether such acts are right in general.

13  Prudentialism is a form of consequentialism claiming that people are entitled to act defensively to avert harm that they think is likely to occur.

14  The 'social contract' is an unspoken agreement by which the citizens of a country adhere to its laws in exchange for protection.

15  Not to be imprisoned without being told the charge against one, so it is possible to organise a defence.

16  Libertarians want a minimum number of laws, just enough to prevent people from harming each other but not to prevent people from participating in dangerous activities that may harm themselves. They do not believe that citizens should be taxed heavily in order to support the jobless through a welfare state.

17  Paternalists believe that the state has a duty to guide its citizens, enforcing laws that prevent people from harming themselves in unhealthy or dangerous pursuits. Critics call this 'the nanny state', suggesting it treats adults as children incapable of making informed choices.

18  Altruism means wishing to help others. Egoism suggests everyone's goal should be to maximise his or her own well-being.

## 8 Analysis

### Now test yourself

1 The first sentence is scene setting. The argument that constitutes the rest of the passage is structurally complete without it. The conclusion is 'Clearly there needs to be a change in the law that currently makes it impossible for us to deport dangerous people who may not receive a fair trial in their own countries.'

2 This passage begins with a sentence of scene setting followed by a reason for intervention and a reason against it, one of which could act as a counter-argument if there was a clear conclusion supported by the other. However, there is no conclusion so it is not an argument. It could easily be made into one if a final sentence were added, such as 'so for the sake of our international reputation it would not be wise for us to intervene'.

### Check your understanding

1 Scene setting.

2 Language used to gain and keep the interest of listeners or readers, such as rhetorical questions.

3 Excessive, exaggerated language used for effect.

4 An emotional assertion of opinion that lacks the structure and careful reasoning of an argument.

5 A distinctive section of an argument, usually consisting of a group of reasons, evidence and examples supporting at least one intermediate conclusion.

6 A move is a switch from one strand of reasoning to another, implying a connection between them.

7 Independent reasons work separately to support a conclusion or intermediate conclusion. Joint reasons work together; if one is taken away the reasoning no longer works.

8 This entails thinking about what would be likely to happen in one scenario or a series of possible scenarios in order to think more clearly about a situation and perhaps make decisions.

## 9 Evaluation

### Now test yourself

1 The form is affirming the consequent, a formal fallacy. It is not necessarily true that Ben passed all his GCSEs. The father did not state that he would let him go to Greece only if he passed them all and he may have been generous if he passed fewer.

### Check your understanding

1 Deductive reasoning uses logic, working out what is certainly true. Inductive reasoning is based on the accumulation of evidence; there is always a chance that new evidence will undermine the conclusion.

2 A premise is the first sentence of the hypothetical argument, e.g. If it rains hard, the washing on the line will get wet. The antecedent is the section before the comma.

3 The consequent is the second part of the premise, the result of the antecedent.

4 Affirming the antecedent.

5 A valid form of reasoning, also known as *modus tollens*.

6 A syllogism.

7 An appeal to authority could strengthen an argument if the authority has specialist knowledge in the field, especially if unchallenged by other authorities. It could fail to strengthen the argument if the authority lacks expertise in the particular field or differs in views from other experts.